Plato Phaedo

Plato Phaedo

Translated by
G.M.A. GRUBE

HACKETT
PUBLISHING
COMPANY, Inc.

G. M. A. GRUBE and the publisher acknowledge with appreciation the extensive help of Richard Hogan and Donald J. Zeyl in correcting and improving this second edition of the *Phaedo*.

Cover design by Richard L. Listenberger
Printed in the United States of America
Second Edition
18 17 16 15 14 13 12   14 15 16

For further information address
Hackett Publishing Company, Inc.,
Box 44937 Indianapolis, Indiana 46244-0937

www.hackettpublishing.com

Library of Congress Cataloging in Publication Data
Plato.
    Plato's Phaedo.
    Includes bibliographical references.
    1. Immortality (Philosophy) I. Grube, G.M.A.
    II. Title
B379.A5G78   184   76-49565
ISBN 0-915144-18-2 pbk.

ISBN-13: 978-0-915144-18-1 (pbk.)

INTRODUCTION

The *Phaedo* professes to be a record of the conversation between Socrates and the friends who have come to visit him in prison on the last day of his life in 399 B.C. But, as with other Platonic dialogues, we can only guess at the date it was written. We can, however, rather confidently place it in relation to other works. Three periods are generally recognized in the writings of Plato: the earliest, which contains the shorter so-called Socratic dialogues and a few of the longer, such as the *Gorgias* and the *Protagoras*; the middle period, which revolves around the *Republic*; and a later period for the more difficult logical and philosophical works. The *Phaedo* shares some characteristics with the first two periods and seems to fit somewhere between the two, after the *Meno* and before the *Republic*, which would seem to date it about 390 B.C. or shortly thereafter.

The personality of Socrates emerges to some extent from all the dialogues, but much less in the last period, until in the *Laws* he does not appear at all. It emerges most vividly in the early period, especially so in those dialogues that are concerned with his trial and imprisonment. In this respect, the *Phaedo* is closely related to the *Apology* and the *Crito*, though it was probably written some years later. On the other hand, the theory of Forms, which is fully developed in the Phaedo, did not appear in the earlier dialogues, a fact that links our dialogue more closely with the second period, and with the *Republic* in particular.

It has often been suggested that the theory of Forms is introduced in the *Phaedo* as a proposition already familiar to Socrates' audience, and in particular to Cebes and Simmias. I think this is very doubtful,[1] but in any case—and more importantly—Plato clearly does not expect his readers to be familiar with it, for the theory is more fully explained here than in any other dialogue, and the explanation is very gradual; each time the theory is introduced a different aspect of it is empha-

1

sized. At 65–66a we learn that there are realities which the soul or mind can only grasp by itself, without interference from the body; in 72e–76c we are told that the human mind or soul had knowledge of these Forms before birth and is reminded of them as a result of sense perceptions, as the particulars imitate the Forms. This is what we call learning, which is really recollection. In 78c–80b the absolute immutability of the Forms is recognized, and their nature contrasted with the physical world. In 100b–e participation in the Forms is the cause of phenomena and of their qualities, but the nature of this participation is left vague and unexplained. In 102d–105b there is further discussion of participation, and a distinction made between properties and accidents is derived from it.

The technical vocabulary is also gradually developed, and it should be noted that the terms *eidos* and *idea* are not used of the Forms until 103b, when the explanation has been completed. Thereafter, they are used freely.[2]

The fully developed theory of Forms links our dialogue with the *Republic*. On the other hand, its psychology or theory of the soul is very different, simpler and less sophisticated. In the first place, we note that the soul in the *Phaedo* is a noncomposite unity, and this is empha-sized and indeed is used to support the argument for its immortality (78cff), and we soon find that the soul is in fact the mind or intellect only. All passions, pleasures and pains, as well as the senses, are classed under body. The struggle between body and soul is expressed in the strongest terms. The soul is the part of man that can apprehend the Forms, and the aim of the philosopher is to "purify" his soul by free-ing it as far as possible from any bodily interference, in order to attain knowledge of true reality, that is, of the Forms. Indeed, this purifica-tion cannot be fully attained until the separation is complete after death, when the immortal soul, alone and by itself, is able to acquire that knowledge. The *Phaedo* is the one dialogue against which the accusation of pure intellectualism and neglect of emotion can be made with some justification. This was undoubtedly due to the influence of the Orphics, who laid great stress on the immortality of the soul, and of the Pythagoreans' idea of the purification of the soul, through exercise of the intellect.

In the *Republic*, we have the same essential struggle for reason to control the life of man, but it is expressed very differently. There, the soul has three parts, namely, the reasonable part, the feelings or spirited part (anger, indignation, and the like), and the passionate part. Whereas in the *Phaedo* the soul is mind or intellect only, and everything else is body, in the *Republic* the soul absorbs everything that is not pure physical sensation. The struggle now becomes one between different parts of the individual soul. Moreover, each part of the soul has its own desires and its own pleasures, and the aim now becomes harmony among the different parts, always under the direction of reason, which remains the noblest part of man, the only part that can acquire knowledge of the Forms and, apparently, the only part that is immortal.[3]

The myth of the *Phaedo* has two themes: the first is that we live in a hollow of the earth and are ignorant of the splendour of its real surface and of the purer life there; and the second describes what happens to immortal souls after death. Both themes are taken up again in the *Republic*, where they are much more vividly and artistically elaborated, the first in the parable of the prisoners in the cave at the beginning of the seventh book, the second in the myth of Er at the end of the tenth book, which completes the whole work.

The concluding pages of the *Phaedo*, in which we see Socrates drinking the hemlock, are the culminating point of the dialogue and of Plato's picture of Socrates' personality. We have been repeatedly told how and why the philosopher should face death without fear or apprehension—indeed, welcome it with a beautiful hope—and here we see him do precisely that. It is an unforgettable passage, one which no one can read without being emotionally affected, however often he may have read it previously. Its beauty is largely due to the utter simplicity of style which only a very great writer can use to such effect. Any further comment would be superfluous.

---

1. See my *Plato's Thought* (Indianapolis: Hackett, 1980), Appendix I, pp. 291–4, and references there. For the opposite view, see R. Hackforth, *Plato's Phaedo* (Cambridge: Cambridge University Press, 1955), p.50.

2. Contrast the manner in which the theory of Forms is introduced in the *Republic* (V, 475e ff), where Glaucon *is* familiar with it, and the word *eidos* is used immediately.

3. *Republic* X, 611b–612a.

Note: Except in rare instances, the translation follows Burnet's Oxford text. The only liberty taken is where the answers to Socrates' questions are very brief, merely indicating assent or the like. In such cases I have replaced "he said," the so frequent repetition of which reads awkwardly in English, by a dash, to indicate a change of speaker.

PHAEDO

ECHECRATES: Were you with Socrates yourself, Phaedo,[1] on the day when he drank the poison in prison, or did someone else tell you about it?

PHAEDO: I was there myself, Echecrates.

E: What are the things he said before he died? And how did he die? I should be glad to hear this. Hardly anyone from Phlius[2] visits Athens nowadays, nor has any stranger come from Athens for some time who could give us a clear account of what happened, except that he drank the poison and died, but nothing more.

P: Did you not even hear how the trial went?

E: Yes, someone did tell us about that, and we wondered that he seems to have died a long time after the trial took place. Why was that, Phaedo?

P: That was by chance, Echecrates. The day before the trial, as it happened, the prow of the ship that the Athenians send to Delos had been crowned with garlands.

E: What ship is that?

P: It is the ship in which, the Athenians say, Theseus once sailed

---

1. Phaedo was a young friend of Socrates who later founded a school of philosophy at Elis.

2. Phlius was a community in the northeastern part of the Pelopponesus where a Pythagorean society flourished about this time. We are told by Diogenes Laertius (early third century A.D.) that Echecrates was a member of that society.

to Crete, taking with him the two lots of seven victims.[3] He saved them
and was himself saved. They vowed then to Apollo, so the story goes,
that if they were saved they would send a mission to Delos every year.
And from that time to this they send such an annual mission to the
god. They have a law to keep the city pure while it lasts, and no execution may take place once the mission has begun until the ship has
made its journey to Delos and returned to Athens, and this can sometimes take a long time if the winds delay it. The mission begins when
the priest of Apollo crowns the prow of the ship, and this happened, as
I say, the day before Socrates' trial. That is why Socrates was in prison
a long time between his trial and his execution.

E: What about his actual death, Phaedo? What did he say? What
did he do? Who of his friends were with him? Or did the authorities not
allow them to be present and he died with no friends present?

P: By no means. Some were present, in fact, a good many.

E: Please be good enough to tell us all that occurred as fully as
possible, unless you have some pressing business.

P: I have the time and I will try to tell you the whole story, for
nothing gives me more pleasure than to call Socrates to mind, whether
talking about him myself, or listening to someone else do so.

E: Your hearers will surely be like you in this, Phaedo. So do try
to tell us every detail as exactly as you can.

P: I certainly found being there an astonishing experience.
Although I was witnessing the death of one who was my friend, I had no
feeling of pity, for the man appeared happy in both manner and words
as he died nobly and without fear, Echecrates, so that it struck me that
even in going down to the underworld he was going with the gods'
blessing and that he would fare well when he got there, if anyone ever
does. That is why I had no feeling of pity, such as would seem natural
in my sorrow, nor indeed of pleasure, as we engaged in philosophical
discussion as we were accustomed to do—for our arguments were of
that sort—but I had a strange feeling, an unaccustomed mixture of
pleasure and pain at the same time as I reflected that he was just about
to die. All of us present were affected in much the same way, sometimes

---

3. Legend says that Minos, king of Crete, compelled the Athenians to send seven
youths and seven maidens every year to be sacrifieced to the Minotaur until Theseus
saved them and killed the monster.

laughing, then weeping; especially one of us, Apollodorus—you know the man and his ways.

E: Of course I do.   b

P: He was quite overcome; but I was myself disturbed, and so were the others.

E: Who, Phaedo, were those present?

P: Among the local people there was Apollodorus, whom I mentioned, Critoboulos and his father,[4] also Hermogenes, Epigenes, Aeschines and Antisthenes. Ctesippus of Paeane was there, Menexenus and some others. Plato, I believe, was ill.[5]

E: Were there some foreigners present?

P: Yes, Simmias from Thebes with Cebes and Phaidondes, and   c from Megara, Euclides and Terpsion.

E: What about Aristippus and Cleombrotus? Were they there?

P: No. They were said to be in Aegina.

E: Was there anyone else?

P: I think these were about all.

E: Well then, what do you say the conversation was about?

P: I will try to tell you everything from the beginning. On the previous days also both the others and I used to visit Socrates. We foregathered at daybreak at the court where the trial took place, for it   d was close to the prison, and each day we used to wait around talking until the prison should open, for it did not open early. When it opened we used to go in to Socrates and spend most of the day with him. On

---

4. The father of Critoboulos is Crito, who in the dialogue named after him tries to persuade Socrates to escape from jail. He is also mentioned in *Apology* 33d and plays a prominent part in the death scene at the end of this dialogue. Several of the other friends of Socrates mentioned here also appear in other dialogues. Hermogenes is one of the speakers in the *Cratylus*. Epigenes is mentioned in *Apology* 33d, as is Aeschines. Aeschines was a writer of Socratic dialogues. Menexenus has a part in the *Lysis* and has a dialogue named after him; Ctesippus appears in both *Lysis* and *Euthydemus*. Simmias and Cebes are mentioned in the *Crito*, 45b, as having come to Athens with enough money to secure Socrates' escape.

5. It is interesting to note that Plato makes it clear that he was *not* present on the last day of Socrates' life, whereas in the *Apology* he twice mentions (34a and 38b) that he *was* present at the trial. Whether this has any significance as regards the historical accuracy of the two works is anyone's guess. Probably it just happened to be so, but these are the only instances in which Plato mentions himself in all his works.

e this day we gathered rather early, because when we left the prison on the previous evening we were informed that the ship from Delos had arrived, and so we told each other to come to the usual place as early as possible. When we arrived the gatekeeper who used to answer our knock came out and told us to wait and not go in until he told us to. "The Eleven,"[6] he said, "are freeing Socrates from his bonds and tell-ing him how his death will take place today." After a short time he

60 came and told us to go in. We found Socrates recently released from his chains, and Xanthippe—you know her—sitting by him, holding their baby. When she saw us, she cried out and said the sort of thing that women usually say: "Socrates, this is the last time your friends will talk to you and you to them." Socrates looked at Crito. "Crito," he said, "let someone take her home." And some of Crito's people led her

b away lamenting and beating her breast.

Socrates sat up on the bed, bent his leg and rubbed it with his hand, and as he rubbed he said: "What a strange thing that which men call pleasure seems to be, and how astonishing the relation it has with what is thought to be its opposite, namely pain! A man cannot have both at the same time. Yet if he pursues and catches the one, he is almost always bound to catch the other also, like two creatures with one head. I think that if Aesop had noted this he would have composed a fable

c that a god wished to reconcile their opposition but could not do so, so he joined their two heads together, and therefore when a man has the one, the other follows later. This seems to be happening to me. My bonds caused pain in my leg, and now pleasure seems to be following."

Cebes intervened and said: "By Zeus, yes, Socrates, you did well to remind me. Evenus[7] asked me the day before yesterday, as others had

d done before, what induced you to write poetry after you came to prison, you who had never composed any poetry before, putting the fables of Aesop into verse and composing the hymn to Apollo. If it is of any concern to you that I should have an answer to give to Evenus when he repeats his question, as I know he will, tell me what to say to him."

Tell him the truth, Cebes, he said, that I did not do this with the idea of rivalling him or his poems, for I knew that would not be easy, but I tried to find out the meaning of certain dreams and to satisfy my

e conscience in case it was this kind of art they were frequently bidding

---

6. The Eleven were the police commissioners of Athens.

7. Socrates refers to Evenus as a Sophist and teacher of the young in *Apology* 20a–b.

me to practise. The dreams were something like this: the same dream often came to me in the past, now in one shape now in another, but saying the same thing: "Socrates," it said, "practise and cultivate the arts." In the past I imagined that it was instructing and advising me to do what I was doing, such as those who encourage runners in a race, that the dream was thus bidding me do the very thing I was doing, namely, to practise the art of philosophy, this being the highest kind of art, and I was doing that. 61

But now, after my trial took place, and the festival of the god was preventing my execution, I thought that, in case my dream was bidding me to practise this popular art, I should not disobey it but compose poetry. I thought it safer not to leave here until I had satisfied my conscience by writing poems in obedience to the dream. So I first b wrote in honour of the god of the present festival. After that I realized that a poet, if he is to be a poet, must compose fables, not arguments. Being no teller of fables myself, I took the stories I knew and had at hand, the fables of Aesop, and I versified the first ones I came across. Tell this to Evenus, Cebes, wish him well and bid him farewell, and tell him, if he is wise, to follow me as soon as possible. I am leaving today, it seems, as the Athenians so order it. c

Said Simmias: "What kind of advice is this you are giving to Evenus, Socrates? I have met him many times, and from my observation he is not at all likely to follow it willingly."

How so, said he, is Evenus not a philosopher?

I think so, Simmias said.

Then Evenus will be willing, like every man who partakes worthily of philosophy. Yet perhaps he will not take his own life, for that, they say, is not right. As he said this, Socrates put his feet on the ground and remained in this position during the rest of the conversation. d

Then Cebes asked: "How do you mean, Socrates, that it is not right to do oneself violence, and yet that the philosopher will be willing to follow one who is dying?"

Come now, Cebes, have you and Simmias, who keep company with Philolaus,[8] not heard about such things?

---

8. Philolaus was a contemporary Pythagorean. The reference to him here, as well as the fact that the story is told to Echecrates at Phlius, gives the whole dialogue a Pythagorean background, and this seems a recognition on Plato's part of Pythagorean influence regarding the theories that follow, in particular, the theory of Forms and the purification of man's eternal soul through intellectual activity.

Nothing definite, Socrates.

Indeed, I too speak about this from hearsay, but I do not mind telling you what I have heard, for it is perhaps most appropriate for one who is about to depart yonder to tell and examine tales about what we believe that journey to be like. What else could one do in the time we have until sunset?

But whatever is the reason, Socrates, for people to say that it is not right to kill oneself? As to your question just now, I have heard Philolaus say this when staying in Thebes and I have also heard it from others, but I have never heard anyone give a clear account of the matter.

Well, he said, we must do our best, and you may yet hear one. And it may well astonish you if this subject, alone of all things, is simple, and it is never, as with everything else, better at certain times and for certain people to die than to live. And if this is so, you may well find it astonishing that those for whom it is better to die are wrong to help themselves, and that they must wait for someone else to benefit them.

And Cebes, lapsing into his own dialect, laughed quietly and said: "Zeus knows it is."

Indeed, said Socrates, it does seem unreasonable when put like that, but perhaps there is reason to it. There is the explanation that is put in the language of the mysteries, that we men are in a kind of prison, and that one must not free oneself or run away. That seems to me an impressive doctrine and one not easy to understand fully. However, Cebes, this seems to me well expressed, that the gods are our guardians and that men are one of their possessions. Or do you not think so?

I do, said Cebes.

And would you not be angry if one of your possessions killed itself when you had not given any sign that you wished it to die, and if you had any punishment you could inflict, you would inflict it?

Certainly, he said.

Perhaps then, put in this way, it is not unreasonable that one should not kill oneself before a god had indicated some necessity to do so, like the necessity now put upon us.

That seems likely, said Cebes. As for what you were saying, that philosophers should be willing and ready to die, that seems strange, Socrates, if what we said just now is reasonable, namely, that a god is our protector and that we are his possessions. It is not logical that the wisest of men should not resent leaving this service in which they are governed by the best of masters, the gods, for a wise man cannot believe that he will look after himself better when he is free. A foolish man might easily think so, that he must escape from his master; he would not reflect that one must not escape from a good master but stay with him as long as possible, because it would be foolish to escape. But the sensible man would want always to remain with one better than himself. So, Socrates, the opposite of what was said before is likely to be true; the wise would resent dying, whereas the foolish would rejoice at it.

I thought that when Socrates heard this he was pleased by Cebes' argumentation. Glancing at us, he said: "Cebes is always on the track of some arguments; he is certainly not willing to be at once convinced by what one says."

Said Simmias: "But actually, Socrates, I think myself that Cebes has a point now. Why should truly wise men want to avoid the service of masters better than themselves, and leave them easily? And I think Cebes is aiming his argument at you, because you are bearing leaving us so lightly, and leaving those good masters, as you say yourself, the gods."

You are both justified in what you say, and I think you mean that I must make a defence against this, as if I were in court.

You certainly must, said Simmias.

Come then, he said, let me try to make my defence to you more convincing than it was to the jury. For, Simmias and Cebes, I should be wrong not to resent dying if I did not believe that I should go first to other wise and good gods, and then to men who have died and are better than men are here. Be assured that, as it is, I expect to join the company of good men. This last I would not altogether insist on, but if I insist on anything at all in these matters, it is that I shall come to gods who are very good masters. That is why I am not so resentful, because I have good hope that some future awaits men after death, as we have been told for years, a much better future for the good than for the wicked.

Well now, Socrates, said Simmias, do you intend to keep this belief to yourself as you leave us, or would you share it with us? I certainly think it would be a blessing for us too, and at the same time it would be your defence if you convince us of what you say.

I will try, he said, but first let us see what it is that Crito here has, I think, been wanting to say for quite a while.

What else, Socrates, said Crito, but what the man who is to give you the poison has been telling me for some time, that I should warn you to talk as little as possible. People get heated when they talk, he says, and one should not be heated when taking the poison, as those who do must sometimes drink it two or three times.

Socrates replied: "Take no notice of him; only let him be prepared to administer it twice or, if necessary, three times."

I was rather sure you would say that, Crito said, but he has been bothering me for some time.

Let him be, he said. I want to make my argument before you, my judges, as to why I think that a man who has truly spent his life in philosophy is probably right to be of good cheer in the face of death and to be very hopeful that after death he will attain the greatest blessings yonder. I will try to tell you, Simmias and Cebes, how this may be so. I am afraid that other people do not realize that the one aim of those who practise philosophy in the proper manner is to practise for dying and death. Now if this is true, it would be strange indeed if they were eager for this all their lives and then resent it when what they have wanted and practised for a long time comes upon them.

Simmias laughed and said: "By Zeus, Socrates, you made me laugh, though I was in no laughing mood just now. I think that the majority, on hearing this, will think that it describes the philosophers very well, and our people in Thebes would thoroughly agree that philosophers are nearly dead and that the majority of men is well aware that they deserve to be.

And they would be telling the truth, Simmias, except for their being aware. They are not aware of the way true philosophers are nearly dead, nor of the way they deserve to be, nor of the sort of death they deserve. But never mind them, he said, let us talk among ourselves. Do we believe that there is such a thing as death?

Certainly, said Simmias.

Is it anything else than the separation of the soul from the body? Do we believe that death is this, namely, that the body comes to be separated by itself apart from the soul, and the soul comes to be separated by itself apart from the body? Is death anything else than that?

No, that is what it is, he said.

Consider then, my good sir, whether you share my opinion, for this will lead us to a better knowledge of what we are investigating. Do you think it is the part of a philosopher to be concerned with such so-called pleasures as those of food and drink?

By no means.

What about the pleasures of sex?

Not at all.

What of the other pleasures concerned with the service of the body? Do you think such a man prizes them greatly, the acquisition of distinguished clothes and shoes and the other bodily ornaments? Do you think he values these or despises them, except in so far as one cannot do without them?

e

I think the true philosopher despises them.

Do you not think, he said, that in general such a man's concern is not with the body but that, as far as he can, he turns away from the body towards the soul?

I do.

So in the first place, such things show clearly that the philosopher more than other men frees the soul from association with the body as much as possible?

65

Apparently.

A man who finds no pleasure in such things and has no part in them is thought by the majority not to deserve to live and to be close to death; the man, that is, who does not care for the pleasures of the body.

What you say is certainly true.

Then what about the actual acquiring of knowledge? Is the body an obstacle when one associates with it in the search for knowledge? I mean, for example, do men find any truth in sight or hearing, or are not even the poets[9] forever telling us that we do not see or hear anything accurately, and surely if those two physical senses are not clear or precise, our other senses can hardly be accurate, as they are all inferior to these. Do you not think so?

b

I certainly do, he said.

When then, he asked, does the soul grasp the truth? For whenever it attempts to examine anything with the body, it is clearly deceived by it.

True.

---

9. "Even the poets" because poetry concerns itself with the world of sense and appeals to the passions and emotions of the lowest part of the soul in the *Republic* (595a ff.), whereas in the *Phaedo* passions and emotions are attributed to the body.

Is it not in reasoning if anywhere that any reality becomes clear to the soul?

Yes.

And indeed the soul reasons best when none of these senses troubles it, neither hearing nor sight, nor pain nor pleasure, but when it is most by itself, taking leave of the body and as far as possible having no contact or association with it in its search for reality.

That is so.

And it is then that the soul of the philosopher most disdains the
d   body, flees from it and seeks to be by itself?

It appears so.

What about the following, Simmias? Do we say that there is such a thing as the Just itself, or not?

We do say so, by Zeus.

And the Beautiful, and the Good?

Of course.

And have you ever seen any of these things with your eyes?

In no way, he said.

Or have you ever grasped them with any of your bodily senses? I am speaking of all things such as Bigness, Health, Strength and, in a word, the reality of all other things, that which each of them essentially is. Is
e   what is most true in them contemplated through the body, or is this the position: whoever of us prepares himself best and most accurately to grasp that thing itself which he is investigating will come closest to the knowledge of it?

Obviously.

Then he will do this most perfectly who approaches the object with thought alone, without associating any sight with his thought, or drag-
66   ging in any sense perception with his reasoning, but who, using pure thought alone, tries to track down each reality pure and by itself, free-ing himself as far as possible from eyes and ears and, in a word, from the whole body, because the body confuses the soul and does not allow it to acquire truth and wisdom whenever it is associated with it. Will not that man reach reality, Simmias, if anyone does?

What you say, said Simmias, is indeed true.

b   All these things will necessarily make the true philosophers believe and say to each other something like this: "There is likely to be some-thing such as a path to guide us out of our confusion, because as long

as we have a body and our soul is fused with such an evil we shall never adequately attain what we desire, which we affirm to be the truth. The body keeps us busy in a thousand ways because of its need for nurture. Moreover, if certain diseases befall it, they impede our search for the truth. It fills us with wants, desires, fears, all sorts of illu-   c
sions and much nonsense, so that, as it is said, in truth and in fact no thought of any kind ever comes to us from the body. Only the body and its desires cause war, civil discord and battles, for all wars are due to the desire to acquire wealth, and it is the body and the care of it, to which we are enslaved, which compel us to acquire wealth, and all   d
this makes us too busy to practise philosophy. Worst of all, if we do get some respite from it and turn to some investigation, everywhere in our investigations the body is present and makes for confusion and fear, so that it prevents us from seeing the truth.

It really has been shown to us that, if we are ever to have pure knowledge, we must escape from the body and observe things in themselves with the soul by itself. It seems likely that we shall, only   e
then, when we are dead, attain that which we desire and of which we claim to be lovers, namely, wisdom, as our argument shows, not while we live; for if it is impossible to attain any pure knowledge with the body, then one of two things is true: either we can never attain knowl-edge or we can do so after death. Then and not before, the soul is by itself apart from the body. While we live, we shall be closest to knowl-   67
edge if we refrain as much as possible from association with the body and do not join with it more than we must, if we are not infected with its nature but purify ourselves from it until the god himself frees us. In this way we shall escape the contamination of the body's folly; we shall be likely to be in the company of people of the same kind, and by our own efforts we shall know all that is pure, which is presumably the truth, for it is not permitted to the impure to attain the pure."   b

Such are the things, Simmias, that all those who love learning in the proper manner must say to one another and believe. Or do you not think so?

I certainly do, Socrates.

And if this is true, my friend, said Socrates, there is good hope that on arriving where I am going, if anywhere, I shall acquire what has been our chief preoccupation in our past life, so that the journey that is now ordered for me is full of good hope, as it is also for any other   c
man who believes that his mind has been prepared and, as it were, purified.

It certainly is, said Simmias.

And does purification not turn out to be what we mentioned in our argument some time ago, namely, to separate the soul as far as possible from the body and accustom it to gather itself and collect itself out of every part of the body and to dwell by itself as far as it can both now and in the future, freed, as it were, from the bonds of the body?

Certainly, he said.

And that freedom and separation of the soul from the body is called death?

That is altogether so.

It is only those who practise philosophy in the right way, we say, who always most want to free the soul; and this release and separation of the soul from the body is the preoccupation of the philosophers?

So it appears.

Therefore, as I said at the beginning, it would be ridiculous for a man to train himself in life to live in a state as close to death as possible, and then to resent it when it comes?

Ridiculous, of course.

In fact, Simmias, he said, those who practise philosophy in the right way are in training for dying and they fear death least of all men. Consider it from this point of view: if they are altogether estranged from the body and desire to have their soul by itself, would it not be quite absurd for them to be afraid and resentful when this happens? If they did not gladly set out for a place, where, on arrival, they may hope to attain that for which they had yearned during their lifetime, that is, wisdom, and where they would be rid of the presence of that from which they are estranged?

Many men, at the death of their lovers, wives or sons, were willing to go to the underworld, driven by the hope of seeing there those for whose company they longed, and being with them. Will then a true lover of wisdom, who has a similar hope and knows that he will never find it to any extent except in Hades, be resentful of dying and not gladly undertake the journey thither? One must surely think so, my friend, if he is a true philosopher, for he is firmly convinced that he will not find pure knowledge anywhere except there. And if this is so, then, as I said just now, would it not be highly unreasonable for such a man to fear death?

It certainly would, by Zeus, he said.

Then you have sufficient indication, he said, that any man whom you see resenting death was not a lover of wisdom but a lover of the body, and also a lover of wealth or of honours, either or both.   c

It is certainly as you say.

And, Simmias, he said, does not what is called courage belong especially to men of this disposition?

Most certainly.

And the quality of moderation which even the majority call by that name, that is, not to get swept off one's feet by one's passions, but to treat them with disdain and orderliness, is this not suited only to those who most of all despise the body and live the life of philosophy?   d

Necessarily so, he said.

If you are willing to reflect on the courage and moderation of other people, you will find them strange.

In what way, Socrates?

You know that they all consider death a great evil?

Definitely, he said.

And the brave among them face death, when they do, for fear of greater evils?

That is so.

Therefore, it is fear and terror that make all men brave, except the philosophers. Yet it is illogical to be brave through fear and cowardice.

It certainly is.   e

What of the moderate among them? Is their experience not similar? Is it licence of a kind that makes them moderate? We say this is impossible, yet their experience of this unsophisticated moderation turns out to be similar: they fear to be deprived of other pleasures which they desire, so they keep away from some pleasures because they are overcome by others. Now to be mastered by pleasure is what they call licence, but what happens to them is that they master certain pleasures because they are mastered by others. This is like what we mentioned   69 just now, that in some way it is a kind of licence that has made them moderate.

That seems likely.

My good Simmias, I fear this is not the right exchange to attain virtue, to exchange pleasures for pleasures, pains for pains and fears for fears, the greater for the less like coins, but that the only valid currency for which all these things should be exchanged is wisdom. With this   b we have real courage and moderation and justice and, in a word, true virtue, with wisdom, whether pleasures and fears and all such things be present or absent. When these are exchanged for one another in separation from wisdom, such virtue is only an illusory appearance of virtue; it is in fact fit for slaves, without soundness or truth, whereas, in truth, moderation and courage and justice are a purging away of

c all such things, and wisdom itself is a kind of cleansing or purification. It is likely that those who established the mystic rites for us were not inferior persons but were speaking in riddles long ago when they said that whoever arrives in the underworld uninitiated and unsanctified will wallow in the mire, whereas he who arrives there purified and initiated will dwell with the gods. There are indeed, as those concerned with the

d mysteries say, many who carry the thyrsus but the Bacchants are few.[10] These latter are, in my opinion, no other than those who have practised philosophy in the right way. I have in my life left nothing undone in order to be counted among these as far as possible, as I have been eager to be in every way. Whether my eagerness was right and we accomplished anything we shall, I think, know for certain in a short time, god willing, on arriving yonder.

This is my defence, Simmias and Cebes, that I am likely to be right to leave you and my masters here without resentment or complaint,

e believing that there, as here, I shall find good masters and good friends. If my defence is more convincing to you than to the Athenian jury, it will be well.

When Socrates finished, Cebes intervened: Socrates, he said, everything else you said is excellent, I think, but men find it very hard to

70 believe what you said about the soul. They think that after it has left the body it no longer exists anywhere, but that it is destroyed and dissolved on the day the man dies, as soon as it leaves the body; and that, on leaving it, it is dispersed like breath or smoke, has flown away and gone and is no longer anything anywhere. If indeed it gathered itself together and existed by itself and escaped those evils you were recently enumerating, there would then be much good hope, Socrates, that

b what you say is true; but to believe this requires a good deal of faith and persuasive argument, to believe that the soul still exists after a man has died and that it still possesses some capability and intelligence."

What you say is true, Cebes, Socrates said, but what shall we do? Do you want to discuss whether this is likely to be true or not?

---

10. That is, the true worshippers of Dionysus, as opposed to those who only carry the external symbols of his worship.

Personally, said Cebes, I should like to hear your opinion on the subject.

I do not think, said Socrates, that anyone who heard me now, not even a comic poet, could say that I am babbling and discussing things that do not concern me, so we must examine the question thoroughly, if you think we should do so. Let us examine it in some such a manner as this: whether the souls of men who have died exist in the underworld or not. We recall an ancient theory that souls arriving there come from here, and then again that they arrive here and are born here from the dead. If that is true, that the living come back from the dead, then surely our souls must exist there, for they could not come back if they did not exist, and this is a sufficient proof that these things are so if it truly appears that the living never come from any other source than from the dead. If this is not the case we should need another argument.

Quite so, said Cebes.

Do not, he said, confine yourself to humanity if you want to understand this more readily, but take all animals and all plants into account, and, in short, for all things which come to be, let us see whether they come to be in this way, that is, from their opposites if they have such, as the beautiful is the opposite of the ugly and the just of the unjust, and a thousand other things of the kind. Let us examine whether those that have an opposite must necessarily come to be from their opposite and from nowhere else, as for example when something comes to be larger it must necessarily become larger from having been smaller before.

Yes.

Then if something smaller comes to be, it will come from something larger before, which became smaller?

That is so, he said.

And the weaker comes to be from the stronger, and the swifter from the slower?

Certainly.

Further, if something worse comes to be, does it not come from the better, and the juster from the more unjust?

Of course.

So we have sufficiently established that all things come to be in this way, opposites from opposites?

Certainly.

c

d

e

71

There is a further point, something such as this, about these opposites: between each of those pairs of opposites there are two processes: from the one to the other and then again from the other to the first; between the larger and the smaller there is increase and decrease, and we call the one increasing and the other decreasing?

Yes, he said.

And so too there is separation and combination, cooling and heating, and all such things, even if sometimes we do not have a name for the process, but in fact it must be everywhere that they come to be from one another, and that there is a process of becoming from each into the other?

Assuredly, he said.

Well then, is there an opposite to living, as sleeping is the opposite of being awake?

Quite so, he said.

What is it?

Being dead, he said.

Therefore, if these are opposites, they come to be from one another, and there are two processes of generation between the two?

Of course.

I will tell you, said Socrates, one of the two pairs I was just talking about, the pair itself and the two processes, and you will tell me the other. I mean, to sleep and to be awake; to be awake comes from sleeping, and to sleep comes from being awake. Of the two processes one is going to sleep, the other is waking up. Do you accept that, or not?

Certainly.

You tell me in the same way about life and death. Do you not say that to be dead is the opposite of being alive?

I do.

And they come to be from one another?

Yes.

What comes to be from being alive?

Being dead.

And what comes to be from being dead?

One must agree that it is being alive.

Then, Cebes, living creatures and things come to be from the dead?

So it appears, he said.

Then our souls exist in the underworld.

That seems likely.

Then in this case one of the two processes of becoming is clear, for dying is clear enough, is it not?

It certainly is.

What shall we do then? Shall we not supply the opposite process of becoming? Is nature to be lame in this case? Or must we provide a process of becoming opposite to dying?

We surely must.

And what is that?

Coming to life again.

Therefore, he said, if there is such a thing as coming to life again, it would be a process of coming from the dead to the living? 72

Quite so.

It is agreed between us then that the living come from the dead in this way no less than the dead from the living and, if that is so, it seems to be a sufficient proof that the souls of the dead must be somewhere whence they can come back again.

I think, Socrates, he said, that this follows from what we have agreed on.

Consider in this way, Cebes, he said, that, as I think, we were not wrong to agree. If the two processes of becoming did not always balance each other as if they were going round in a circle, but generation proceeded from one point to its opposite in a straight line and it did not turn back again to the other opposite or take any turning, do you realize that all things would ultimately have the same form, be affected in the same way, and cease to become? b

How do you mean? he said.

It is not hard to understand what I mean. If, for example, there was such a process as going to sleep, but no corresponding process of waking up, you realize that in the end everything would show the story of Endymion[11] to have no meaning. There would be no point to it c because everything would have the same experience as he and be asleep. And if everything were combined and nothing separated, the saying of

---

11. Endymion was granted eternal sleep by Zeus, in some versions at the request of Selene (the moon).

Anaxagoras[12] would soon be true, "that all things were mixed together."
In the same way, my dear Cebes, if everything that partakes of
life were to die and remain in that state and not come to life again, would
not everything ultimately have to be dead and nothing alive? Even if
the living came from some other source, and all that lived died, how
could all things avoid being absorbed in death?

It could not be, Socrates, said Cebes, and I think what you say is
altogether true.

I think, Cebes, said he, that this is very definitely the case and that
we were not deceived when we agreed on this: coming to life again in
truth exists, the living come to be from the dead, and the souls of the
dead exist.

Furthermore, Socrates, Cebes rejoined, such is also the case if that
theory is true that you are accustomed to mention frequently, that for
us learning is no other than recollection. According to this, we must at
some previous time have learned what we now recollect. This is possible only if our soul existed somewhere before it took on this human
shape. So according to this theory too, the soul is likely to be something
immortal.

Cebes, Simmias interrupted, what are the proofs of this? Remind
me, for I do not quite recall them at the moment.

There is one excellent argument, said Cebes, namely that when
men are interrogated in the right manner, they always give the right
answer of their own accord, and they could not do this if they did not
possess the knowledge and the right explanation inside them. Then
if one shows them a diagram or something else of that kind, this will
show most clearly that such is the case.[13]

If this does not convince you, Simmias, said Socrates, see whether you
agree if we examine it in some such way as this, for do you doubt that
what we call learning is recollection?

It is not that I doubt, said Simmias, but I want to experience the

---

12. Anaxagoras of Clazomenae was born at the beginning of the fifth century B.C.
He came to Athens as a young man and spent most of his life there in the study of
natural philosophy. He is quoted later in the dialogue as claiming that the universe is
directed by Mind (Nous). See 97c ff. The reference here is to his statement that in the
original state of the world all its elements were thoroughly commingled.

13. In the *Meno* Socrates does precisely that. By means of a geometrical diagram
and merely by asking Meno's slave questions, he elicits from him the answer that the
square on the diameter of a square is double the original square. There, too, this is
taken to prove that knowledge is recollection.

very thing we are discussing, recollection, and from what Cebes
undertook to say, I am now remembering and am pretty nearly convinced. Nevertheless, I should like to hear now the way you were
intending to explain it.

This way, he said. We surely agree that if anyone recollects anything,
he must have known it before.   c

Quite so, he said.

Do we not also agree that when knowledge comes to mind in this
way, it is recollection? What way do I mean? Like this: when a man sees
or hears or in some other way perceives one thing and not only knows
that thing but also thinks of another thing of which the knowledge is
not the same but different, are we not right to say that he recollects the
second thing that comes into his mind?

How do you mean?   d

Things such as this: to know a man is surely a different knowledge
from knowing a lyre.

Of course.

Well, you know what happens to lovers: whenever they see a lyre, a
garment or anything else that their beloved is accustomed to use, they
know the lyre, and the image of the boy to whom it belongs comes into
their mind. This is recollection, just as someone, on seeing Simmias,
often recollects Cebes, and there are thousands of other such occur-
rences.

Thousands indeed, said Simmias.

Is this kind of thing not recollection of a kind? he said, especially so
when one experiences it about things that one had forgotten, because   e
one had not seen them for some time? — Quite so.

Further, he said, can a man seeing the picture of a horse or a lyre
recollect a man, or seeing a picture of Simmias recollect Cebes? —
Certainly.

Or seeing a picture of Simmias, recollect Simmias himself? — He
certainly can.

In all these cases the recollection can be occasioned by things that are
similar, but it can also be occasioned by things that are dissimilar? — It 74
can.

When the recollection is caused by similar things, must one not of
necessity also experience this: to consider whether the similarity to
that which one recollects is deficient in any respect or complete? —
One must.

Consider, he said, whether this is the case: we say that there is something that is equal. I do not mean a stick equal to a stick or a stone to a stone, or anything of that kind, but something else beyond all these, the Equal itself. Shall we say that this exists or not?

b   Indeed we shall, by Zeus, said Simmias, most definitely.

And do we know what this is?—Certainly.

Whence have we acquired the knowledge of it? Is it not from the things we mentioned just now, from seeing sticks or stones or some other things that are equal we come to think of that other which is different from them? Or doesn't it seem to you to be different? Look at it also this way: do not equal stones and sticks sometimes, while remaining the same, appear to one to be equal and to another to be unequal? — Certainly they do.

But what of the equals themselves?[14] Have they ever appeared unequal to you, or Equality to be Inequality?

c   Never, Socrates.

These equal things and the Equal itself are therefore not the same?

I do not think they are the same at all, Socrates.

But it is definitely from the equal things, though they are different from that Equal, that you have derived and grasped the knowledge of equality?

Very true, Socrates.

Whether it be like them or unlike them?

Certainly.

It makes no difference. As long as the sight of one thing makes you think of another, whether it be similar or dissimilar, this must of necessity be recollection?

d   Quite so.

Well then, he said, do we experience something like this in the case of equal sticks and the other equal objects we just mentioned? Do they seem to us to be equal in the same sense as what is Equal itself? Is there some deficiency in their being such as the Equal, or is there not?

---

14. The plural is puzzling, as only the Form of Equality, on the one hand, and the (imperfectly) equal "sticks and stones" have been mentioned. Commentators suggest that the plural here refers to mathematical equals such as the angles at the base of an isosceles triangle. Plato must have something of the kind in mind, but it is hard to see how he expects a reader who could not be familiar with his later work to realize it, especially as the "equal things" in the next line again refer to the particulars.

A considerable deficiency, he said.

Whenever someone, on seeing something, realizes that that which he now sees wants to be like some other reality but falls short and cannot be like that other since it is inferior, do we agree that the one who thinks this must have prior knowledge of that to which he says it is like, but deficiently so? e

Necessarily.

Well, do we also feel this about the equal objects and the Equal itself, or do we not?

Very definitely.

We must then possess knowledge of the Equal before that time when we first saw the equal objects and realized that all these objects strive to be like the Equal but are deficient in this. 75

That is so.

Then surely we also agree that this conception of ours derives from seeing or touching or some other sense perception, and cannot come into our mind in any other way, for all these senses, I say, are the same.

They are the same, Socrates, at any rate in respect to that which our argument wishes to make plain.

Our sense perceptions must surely make us realize that all that we perceive through them is striving to reach that which is Equal but falls short of it; or how do we express it? b

Like that.

Then before we began to see or hear or otherwise perceive, we must have possessed knowledge of the Equal itself if we were about to refer our sense perceptions of equal objects to it, and realized that all of them were eager to be like it, but were inferior.

That follows from what has been said, Socrates.

But we began to see and hear and otherwise perceive right after birth?

Certainly.

We must then have acquired the knowledge of the Equal before this. c

Yes.

It seems then that we must have possessed it before birth.

It seems so.

Therefore, if we had this knowledge, we knew before birth and immediately after not only the Equal, but the Greater and the Smaller and all such things, for our present argument is no more about the

Equal than about the Beautiful itself, the Good itself, the Just, the Pious
d   and, as I say, about all those things which we mark with the seal of "what it
is," both when we are putting questions and answering them. So we must
have acquired knowledge of them all before we were born.

That is so.

If, having acquired this knowledge in each case, we have not forgotten it, we remain knowing and have knowledge throughout our life,
for to know is to acquire knowledge, keep it and not lose it. Do we not
call the losing of knowledge forgetting?

e   Most certainly, Socrates, he said.

But, I think, if we acquired this knowledge before birth, then lost
it at birth, and then later by the use of our senses in connection with
those objects we mentioned, we recovered the knowledge we had
before, would not what we call learning be the recovery of our own
knowledge, and we are right to call this recollection?

Certainly.

76   It was seen to be possible for someone to see or hear or otherwise
perceive something, and by this to be put in mind of something else
which he had forgotten and which is related to it by similarity or difference. One of two things follows, as I say: either we were born
with the knowledge of it, and all of us know it throughout life, or those
who later, we say, are learning, are only recollecting, and learning
would be recollection.

That is certainly the case, Socrates.

Which alternative do you choose, Simmias? That we are born with
b   this knowledge or that we recollect later the things of which we had
knowledge previously?

I have no means of choosing at the moment, Socrates.

Well, can you make this choice? What is your opinion about it? A
man who has knowledge would be able to give an account of what he
knows, or would he not?

He must certainly be able to do so, Socrates, he said.

And do you think everybody can give an account of the things we
were mentioning just now?

I wish they could, said Simmias, but I'm afraid it is much more likely
that by this time tomorrow there will be no one left who can do so
adequately.

c   So you do not think that everybody has knowledge of those things?

No indeed.

So they recollect what they once learned?

They must.

When did our souls acquire the knowledge of them? Certainly not since we were born as men.

Indeed no.

Before that then?

Yes.

So then, Simmias, our souls also existed apart from the body before they took on human form, and they had intelligence.

Unless we acquire the knowledge at the moment of birth, Socrates, for that time is still left to us.

Quite so, my friend, but at what other time do we lose it? We just now agreed that we are not born with that knowledge. Do we then lose it at the very time we acquire it, or can you mention any other time?

I cannot, Socrates. I did not realize that I was talking nonsense.

So this is our position, Simmias? he said. If those realities we are always talking about exist, the Beautiful and the Good and all that kind of reality, and we refer all the things we perceive to that reality, discovering that it existed before and is ours, and we compare these things with it, then, just as they exist, so our soul must exist before we are born. If these realities do not exist, then this argument is altogether futile. Is this the position, that there is an equal necessity for those realities to exist, and for our souls to exist before we were born? If the former do not exist, neither do the latter?

I do not think, Socrates, said Simmias, that there is any possible doubt that it is equally necessary for both to exist, and it is opportune that our argument comes to the conclusion that our soul exists before we are born, and equally so that reality of which you are now speaking. Nothing is so evident to me personally as that all such things must certainly exist, the Beautiful, the Good, and all those you mentioned just now. I also think that sufficient proof of this has been given.

Then what about Cebes? said Socrates, for we must persuade Cebes also.

He is sufficiently convinced I think, said Simmias, though he is the most difficult of men to persuade by argument, but I believe him to be fully convinced that our soul existed before we were born. I do not think myself, however, that it has been proved that the soul continues to exist after death; the opinion of the majority which Cebes mentioned still stands, that when a man dies his soul is dispersed and this is the end of its existence. What is to prevent the soul coming to be and being constituted from some other source, existing before it enters a human body and then, having done so and departed from it, itself dying and being destroyed?

c   You are right, Simmias, said Cebes. Half of what needed proof has been proved, namely, that our soul existed before we were born, but further proof is needed that it exists no less after we have died, if the proof is to be complete.

It has been proved even now, Simmias and Cebes, said Socrates, if you are ready to combine this argument with the one we agreed on before, that every living thing must come from the dead. If the soul exists before, it must, as it comes to life and birth, come from nowhere

d   else than death and being dead, so how could it avoid existing after death since it must be born again? What you speak of has then even now been proved. However, I think you and Simmias would like to discuss the argument more fully. You seem to have this childish fear that the wind would really dissolve and scatter the soul, as it leaves the

e   body, especially if one happens to die in a high wind and not in calm weather.

Cebes laughed and said: Assuming that we were afraid, Socrates, try to change our minds, or rather do not assume that we are afraid, but perhaps there is a child in us who has these fears; try to persuade him not to fear death like a bogey.

You should, said Socrates, sing a charm over him every day until you have charmed away his fears.

78   Where shall we find a good charmer for these fears, Socrates, he said, now that you are leaving us?

Greece is a large country, Cebes, he said, and there are good men in it; the tribes of foreigners are also numerous. You should search for such a charmer among them all, sparing neither trouble nor expense, for there is nothing on which you could spend your money to greater advantage. You must also search among yourselves, for you might not easily find people who could do this better than yourselves.

That shall be done, said Cebes, but let us, if it pleases you, go back to

b   the argument where we left it.

Of course it pleases me.

Splendid, he said.

We must then ask ourselves something like this: what kind of thing is likely to be scattered? On behalf of what kind of thing should one fear this, and for what kind of thing should one not fear it? We should then examine to which class the soul belongs, and as a result either fear for the soul or be of good cheer.

What you say is true.

Is not anything that is composite and a compound by nature liable c to be split up into its component parts, and only that which is noncomposite, if anything, is not likely to be split up?

I think that is the case, said Cebes.

Are not the things that always remain the same and in the same state most likely not to be composite, whereas those that vary from one time to another and are never the same are composite?

I think that is so.

Let us then return to those same things with which we were dealing earlier, to that reality of whose existence we are giving an account in d our questions and answers; are they ever the same and in the same state, or do they vary from one time to another; can the Equal itself, the Beautiful itself, each thing in itself, the real, ever be affected by any change whatever? Or does each of them that really is, being simple by itself, remain the same and never in any way tolerate any change whatever?

It must remain the same, said Cebes, and in the same state, Socrates.

What of the many beautiful particulars, be they men, horses, clothes, or other such things, or the many equal particulars, and all e those which bear the same name as those others? Do they remain the same or, in total contrast to those other realities, one might say, never in any way remain the same as themselves or in relation to each other?

The latter is the case, they are never in the same state.

These latter you could touch and see and perceive with the other 79 senses, but those that always remain the same can be grasped only by the reasoning power of the mind? They are not seen but are invisible?

That is altogether true, he said.

Do you then want us to assume two kinds of existences, the visible and the invisible?

Let us assume this.

And the invisible always remains the same, whereas the visible never does?

Let us assume that too.

Now one part of ourselves is the body, another part is the soul? b

Quite so.

To which class of existence do we say the body is more alike and akin?

To the visible, as anyone can see.

What about the soul? Is it visible or invisible?

It is not visible to men, Socrates, he said.

Well, we meant visible and invisible to human eyes; or to any others, do you think?

To human eyes.

Then what do we say about the soul? Is it visible or not visible?

Not visible.

So it is invisible?— Yes.

So the soul is more like the invisible than the body, and the body
c   more like the visible? — Without any doubt, Socrates.

Haven't we also said some time ago that when the soul makes use of the body to investigate something, be it through hearing or seeing or some other sense—for to investigate something through the body is to do it through the senses—it is dragged by the body to the things that are never the same, and the soul itself strays and is confused and dizzy, as if it were drunk, in so far as it is in contact with that kind of thing?

Certainly.

d   But when the soul investigates by itself it passes into the realm of what is pure, ever existing, immortal and unchanging, and being akin to this, it always stays with it whenever it is by itself and can do so; it ceases to stray and remains in the same state as it is in touch with things of the same kind, and its experience then is what is called wisdom?

Altogether well said and very true, Socrates, he said.

Judging from what we have said before and what we are saying
e   now, to which of these two kinds do you think that the soul is more alike and more akin?

I think, Socrates, he said, that on this line of argument any man, even the dullest, would agree that the soul is altogether more like that which always exists in the same state rather than like that which does not.

What of the body?

That is like the other.

Look at it also this way: when the soul and the body are together,

nature orders the one to be subject and to be ruled, and the other to 80
rule and be master. Then again, which do you think is like the divine
and which like the mortal? Do you not think that the nature of the
divine is to rule and to lead, whereas it is that of the mortal to be ruled
and be subject?

I do.

Which does the soul resemble?

Obviously, Socrates, the soul resembles the divine, and the body
resembles the mortal.

Consider then, Cebes, whether it follows from all that has been said
that the soul is most like the divine, deathless, intelligible, uniform,
indissoluble, always the same as itself, whereas the body is most like b
that which is human, mortal, multiform, unintelligible, soluble and
never consistently the same. Have we anything else to say to show, my
dear Cebes, that this is not the case?

We have not.

Well then, that being so, is it not natural for the body to dissolve
easily, and for the soul to be altogether indissoluble, or nearly so?

Of course. c

You realize, he said, that when a man dies, the visible part, the
body, which exists in the visible world, and which we call the corpse,
whose natural lot it would be to dissolve, fall apart and be blown away,
does not immediately suffer any of these things but remains for a fair
time, in fact, quite a long time if the man dies with his body in a suit-
able condition and at a favourable season? If the body is emaciated
or embalmed, as in Egypt, it remains almost whole for a remarkable
length of time, and even if the body decays, some parts of it, namely
bones and sinews and the like, are nevertheless, one might say, death- d
less. Is that not so? — Yes.

Will the soul, the invisible part which makes its way to a region of
the same kind, noble and pure and invisible, to Hades in fact, to the
good and wise god whither, god willing, my soul must soon be going—
will the soul, being of this kind and nature, be scattered and destroyed
on leaving the body, as the majority of men say? Far from it, my dear
Cebes and Simmias, but what happens is much more like this: if it is e
pure when it leaves the body and drags nothing bodily with it, as it
had no willing association with the body in life, but avoided it and
gathered itself together by itself and always practised this, which is no
other than practising philosophy in the right way, in fact, training to 81

die easily. Or is this not training for death?

It surely is.

A soul in this state makes its way to the invisible, which is like itself, the divine and immortal and wise, and arriving there it can be happy, having rid itself of confusion, ignorance, fear, violent desires and the other human ills and, as is said of the initiates, truly spend the rest of time with the gods. Shall we say this, Cebes, or something different?

This, by Zeus, said Cebes.

b   But I think that if the soul is polluted and impure when it leaves the body, having always been associated with it and served it, bewitched by physical desires and pleasures to the point at which nothing seems to exist for it but the physical, which one can touch and see or eat and drink or make use of for sexual enjoyment, and if that soul is accustomed to hate and fear and avoid that which is dim and invisible to the eyes but intelligible and to be grasped by philosophy—do you think such a soul will escape pure and by itself?

c   Impossible, he said.

It is no doubt permeated by the physical, which constant intercourse and association with the body, as well as considerable practice, has caused to become ingrained in it?

Quite so.

We must believe, my friend, that this bodily element is heavy, ponderous, earthy and visible. Through it, such a soul has become heavy and is dragged back to the visible region in fear of the unseen and of Hades. It wanders, as we are told, around graves and monuments,

d   where shadowy phantoms, images that such souls produce, have been seen, souls that have not been freed and purified but share in the visible, and are therefore seen.

That is likely, Socrates.

It is indeed, Cebes. Moreover, these are not the souls of good but of inferior men, which are forced to wander there, paying the penalty for their previous bad upbringing. They wander until their longing for

e   that which accompanies them, the physical, again imprisons them in a body, and they are then, as is likely, bound to such characters as they have practised in their life.

What kind of characters do you say these are, Socrates?

Those, for example, who have carelessly practised gluttony, violence and drunkenness are likely to join a company of donkeys or of similar

82   animals. Do you not think so?

Very likely.

Those who have esteemed injustice highly, and tyranny and plunder will join the tribes of wolves and hawks and kites, or where else shall we say that they go?

Certainly to those, said Cebes.

And clearly, the destination of the others will conform to the way in which they have behaved?

Clearly, of course.

The happiest of these, who will also have the best destination, are those who have practised popular and social virtue, which they call moderation and justice and which was developed by habit and practice, without philosophy or understanding? b

How are they the happiest?

Because it is likely that they will again join a social and gentle group, either of bees or wasps or ants, and then again the same kind of human group, and so be moderate men.

That is likely.

No one may join the company of the gods who has not practised philosophy and is not completely pure when he departs from life, no one but the lover of learning. It is for this reason, my friends Simmias c and Cebes, that those who practise philosophy in the right way keep away from all bodily passions, master them and do not surrender themselves to them; it is not at all for fear of wasting their substance and of poverty, which the majority and the money-lovers fear, nor for fear of dishonour and ill repute, like the ambitious and lovers of honours, that they keep away from them.

That would not be natural for them, Socrates, said Cebes.

By Zeus, no, he said. Those who care for their own soul and do not d live for the service of their body dismiss all these things. They do not travel the same road as those who do not know where they are going but, believing that nothing should be done contrary to philosophy and their deliverance and purification, they turn to this and follow wherever philosophy leads.

How so, Socrates?

I will tell you, he said. The lovers of learning know that when philosophy gets hold of their soul, it is imprisoned in and clinging to the body, and that it is forced to examine other things through it as e through a cage and not by itself, and that it wallows in every kind of ignorance. Philosophy sees that the worst feature of this imprisonment is that it is due to desires, so that the prisoner himself is contributing to his own incarceration most of all. As I say, the lovers of learning know that philosophy gets hold of their soul when it is in that state, then gently encourages it and tries to free it by showing them that investigation through the eyes is full of deceit, as is that through the ears and the other senses. Philosophy then persuades the soul to withdraw from the senses in so far as it is not compelled to use them and bids the soul to gather itself together by itself, to trust only itself and whatever reality, existing by itself, the soul by itself understands, and not to consider as true whatever it examines by other means, for this is different in different circumstances and is sensible and visible, whereas what the soul itself sees is intelligible and invisible. The soul of the true philosopher thinks that this deliverance must not be opposed and so keeps away from pleasures and desires and pains as far as he can; he reflects that violent pleasure or pain or passion does not cause merely such evils as one might expect, such as one suffers when one has been sick or extravagant through desire, but the greatest and most extreme evil, though one does not reflect on this.

What is that, Socrates? asked Cebes.

That the soul of every man, when it feel violent pleasure or pain in connection with some object, inevitably believes at the same time that what causes such feelings must be very clear and very true, which it is not. Such objects are mostly visible, are they not?

Certainly.

And doesn't such an experience tie the soul to the body most completely?

How so?

Because every pleasure or pain provides, as it were, another nail to rivet the soul to the body and to weld them together. It makes the soul corporeal, so that it believes that truth is what the body says it is. As it shares the beliefs and delights of the body, I think it inevitably comes to share its ways and manner of life and is unable ever to reach Hades in a pure state; it is always full of body when it departs, so that it soon falls back into another body and grows with it as if it had been sewn into it. Because of this, it can have no part in the company of the divine, the pure and uniform.

What you say is very true, Socrates, said Cebes.

This is why genuine lovers of learning are moderate and brave, or do you think it is for the reasons the majority says they are?

I certainly do not. 84

Indeed no. This is how the soul of a philosopher would reason: it would not think that while philosophy must free it, it should while being freed surrender itself to pleasures and pains and imprison itself again, thus labouring in vain like Penelope at her web. The soul of the philosopher achieves a calm from such emotions; it follows reason and ever stays with it contemplating the true, the divine, which is not the object of opinion. Nurtured by this, it believes that one should live in this manner as long as one is alive and, after death, arrive at what is b akin and of the same kind, and escape from human evils. After such nurture there is no danger, Simmias and Cebes, that one should fear that, on parting from the body, the soul would be scattered and dissipated by the winds and no longer be anything anywhere.

When Socrates finished speaking there was a long silence. He c appeared to be concentrating on what had been said, and so were most of us. But Cebes and Simmias were whispering to each other. Socrates observed them and questioned them. Come, he said, do you think there is something lacking in my argument? There are still many doubtful points and many objections for anyone who wants a thorough discussion of these matters. If you are discussing some other subject, I have nothing to say, but if you have some difficulty about this one, do not hesitate to speak for yourselves and expound it if you think the argument could be improved, and if you think you will do better, take me along with you in the discussion. d

I will tell you the truth, Socrates, said Simmias. Both of us have been in difficulty for some time, and each of us has been urging the other to question you because we wanted to hear what you would say, but we hesitated to bother you, lest it be displeasing to you in your present misfortune.

When Socrates heard this he laughed quietly and said: "Really, Simmias, it would be hard for me to persuade other people that I do not consider my present fate a misfortune if I cannot persuade even e you, and you are afraid that it is more difficult to deal with me than before. You seem to think me inferior to the swans in prophecy. They sing before too, but when they realize that they must die they sing most and most beautifully, as they rejoice that they are about to depart to join the god whose servants they are. But men, because of their own 85 fear of death, tell lies about the swans and say that they lament their death and sing in sorrow. They do not reflect that no bird sings when it is hungry or cold or suffers in any other way, neither the nightin-

gale nor the swallow nor the hoopoe, though they do say that these
sing laments when in pain. Nor do the swans, but I believe that as they
b   belong to Apollo, they are prophetic, have knowledge of the future
and sing of the blessings of the underworld, sing and rejoice on that
day beyond what they did before. As I believe myself to be a fellow ser-
vant with the swans and dedicated to the same god, and have received
from my master a gift of prophecy not inferior to theirs, I am no more
despondent than they on leaving life. Therefore, you must speak and
ask whatever you want as long as the authorities allow it."

Well spoken, said Simmias. I will tell you my difficulty, and then
Cebes will say why he does not accept what was said. I believe, as per-
c   haps you do, that precise knowledge on that subject is impossible
or extremely difficult in our present life, but that it surely shows a
very poor spirit not to examine thoroughly what is said about it, and
to desist before one is exhausted by an all-round investigation. One
should achieve one of these things: learn the truth about these things
or find it for oneself, or, if that is impossible, adopt the best and most
d   irrefutable of men's theories, and, borne upon this, sail through the
dangers of life as upon a raft, unless someone should make that
journey safer and less risky upon a firmer vessel of some divine doctrine. So even now, since you have said what you did, I will feel no
shame at asking questions, and I will not blame myself in the future
because I did not say what I think. As I examine what we said, both by
myself and with Cebes, it does not seem to be adequate.

e   Said Socrates: "You may well be right, my friend, but tell me how it
is inadequate."

In this way, as it seems to me, he said: "One might make the same
argument about harmony, lyre and strings, that a harmony is something invisible, without body, beautiful and divine in the attuned lyre,
86   whereas the lyre itself and its strings are physical, bodily, composite,
earthy and akin to what is mortal. Then if someone breaks the lyre,
cuts or breaks the strings and then insists, using the same argument
as you, that the harmony must still exist and is not destroyed because
it would be impossible for the lyre and the strings, which are mortal,
still to exist when the strings are broken, and for the harmony, which
is akin and of the same nature as the divine and immortal, to be
b   destroyed before that which is mortal; he would say that the harmony
itself still must exist and that the wood and the strings must rot before
the harmony can suffer. And indeed, Socrates, I think you must have
this in mind, that we really do suppose the soul to be something of this

kind; as the body is stretched and held together by the hot and the cold, the dry and the moist and other such things, and our soul is a mixture and harmony of those things when they are mixed with each c other rightly and in due measure. If then the soul is a kind of harmony or attunement, clearly, when our body is relaxed or stretched without due measure by diseases and other evils, the soul must immediately be destroyed, even if it be most divine, as are the other harmonies found in music and all the works of artists, and the remains of each body last for a long time until they rot or are burned. Consider what we shall say in answer to one who deems the soul to be a mixture of bodily ele- d ments and to be the first to perish in the process we call death."

Socrates looked at us keenly, as was his habit, smiled and said: "What Simmias says is quite fair. If one of you is more resourceful than I am, why did he not answer him, for he seems to have handled the argument competently. However, I think that before we answer him, we should hear Cebes' objection, in order that we may have time to e deliberate on an answer. When we have heard him we should either agree with them, if we think them in tune with us or, if not, defend our own argument. Come then, Cebes. What is troubling you?"

I tell you, said Cebes, the argument seems to me to be at the same point as before and open to the same objection. I do not deny that it 87 has been very elegantly and, if it is not offensive to say so, sufficiently proved that our soul existed before it took on this present form, but I do not believe the same applies to its existing somewhere after our death. Not that I agree with Simmias' objection that the soul is not stronger and much more lasting than the body, for I think it is supe- rior in all these respects. "Why then," the argument might say, "are you still unconvinced? Since you see that when the man dies, the weaker part continues to exist, do you not think that the more last- ing part must be preserved during that time?" On this point consider b whether what I say makes sense.

Like Simmias, I too need an image, for I think this argument is much as if one said at the death of an old weaver that the man had not perished but was safe and sound somewhere, and offered as proof the fact that the cloak the old man had woven himself and was wear- ing was still sound and had not perished. If one was not convinced, he c would be asked whether a man lasts longer than a cloak which is in use and being worn, and if the answer was that a man lasts much lon- ger, this would be taken as proof that the man was definitely safe and sound, since the more temporary thing had not perished. But Simmias,

I do not think that is so, for consider what I say. Anybody could see that the man who said this was talking nonsense. That weaver had woven and worn out many such cloaks. He perished after many of them, but before the last. That does not mean that a man is inferior and weaker than a cloak. The image illustrates, I think, the relationship of the soul to the body, and anyone who says the same thing about them would appear to me to be talking sense, that the soul lasts a long time while the body is weaker and more short-lived. He might say that each soul wears out many bodies, especially if it lives many years. If the body were in a state of flux and perished while the man was still alive, and the soul wove afresh the body that is worn out, yet it would be inevitable that whenever the soul perished it would be wearing the last body it wove and perish only before this last. Then when the soul perished, the body would show the weakness of its nature by soon decaying and disappearing. So we cannot trust this argument and be confident that our soul continues to exist somewhere after our death. For, if one were to concede, even more than you do, to a man using that argument, if one were to grant him not only that the soul exists in the time before we are born, but that there is no reason why the soul of some should not exist and continue to exist after our death, and thus frequently be born and die in turn; if one were to grant him that the soul's nature is so strong that it can survive many bodies, but if, having granted all this, one does not further agree that the soul is not damaged by its many births and is not, in the end, altogether destroyed in one of those deaths, he might say that no one knows which death and dissolution of the body brings about the destruction of the soul, since not one of us can be aware of this. And in that case, any man who faces death with confidence is foolish, unless he can prove that the soul is altogether immortal. If he cannot, a man about to die must of necessity always fear for his soul, lest the present separation of the soul from the body bring about the complete destruction of the soul.

When we heard what they said we were all depressed, as we told each other afterwards. We had been quite convinced by the previous argument, and they seemed to confuse us again, and to drive us to doubt not only what had already been said but also what was going to be said, lest we be worthless as critics or the subject itself admitted of no certainty.

ECHECRATES: By the gods, Phaedo, you have my sympathy, for as I listen to you now I find myself saying to myself: "What argument

shall we trust, now that that of Socrates, which was extremely convinc-   d
ing, has now fallen into discredit?" The statement that the soul is some
kind of harmony has a remarkable hold on me, now and always, and
when it was mentioned it reminded me that I had myself previously
thought so. And now I am again quite in need, as if from the beginning,
of some other argument to convince me that the soul does not die along
with the man. Tell me then, by Zeus, how Socrates tackled the argument. Was he obviously distressed, as you say you people were, or was
he not, but quietly came to the rescue of his argument, and did he do   e
so satisfactorily or inadequately? Tell us everything as precisely as you
can.

PHAEDO: I have certainly often admired Socrates, Echecrates, but
never more than on this occasion. That he had a reply was perhaps
not strange. What I wondered at most in him was the pleasant, kind   89
and admiring way he received the young men's argument, and how
sharply he was aware of the effect the discussion had on us, and then
how well he healed our distress and, as it were, recalled us from our
flight and defeat and turned us around to join him in the examination
of their argument.

E: How did he do this?

P: I will tell you. I happened to be sitting on his right by the couch
on a low stool, so that he was sitting well above me. He stroked my
head and pressed the hair on the back of my neck, for he was in the   b
habit of playing with my hair at times. "Tomorrow, Phaedo," he said,
"you will probably cut this beautiful hair."

Likely enough, Socrates, I said.

Not if you take my advice, he said.

Why not? said I.

It is today, he said, that I shall cut my hair and you yours, if our
argument dies on us, and we cannot revive it. If I were you, and the
argument escaped me, I would take an oath, as the Argives[15] did, not   c
to let my hair grow before I fought again and defeated the argument of
Simmias and Cebes.

But, I said, they say that not even Heracles could fight two people.

Then call on me as your Iolaus, as long as the daylight lasts.

---

15. Herodotus (I, 82) tells us that after losing the city of Thyreae to the Spartans,
the Argives swore not to let their hair grow again or their women wear golden ornaments until they had recaptured it.

I shall call on you, but in this case as Iolaus calling on Heracles.

It makes no difference, he said, but first there is a certain experience we must be careful to avoid.

What is that? I asked.

d   That we should not become misologues, as people become misanthropes. There is no greater evil one can suffer than to hate reasonable discourse. Misology and misanthropy arise in the same way. Misanthropy comes when a man without knowledge or skill has placed great trust in someone and believes him to be altogether truthful, sound and trustworthy; then, a short time afterwards he finds him to be wicked and unreliable, and then this happens in another case; when one has frequently had that experience, especially with those whom
e   one believed to be one's closest friends, then, in the end, after many such blows, one comes to hate all men and to believe that no one is sound in any way at all. Have you not seen this happen?

I surely have, I said.

This is a shameful state of affairs, he said, and obviously due to an attempt to have human relations without any skill in human affairs, for such skill would lead one to believe, what is in fact true, that the very
90   good and the very wicked are both quite rare, and that most men are between those extremes.

How do you mean? said I.

The same as with the very tall and the very short, he said. Do you think anything is rarer than to find an extremely tall man or an extremely short one? Or a dog or anything else whatever? Or again, one extremely swift or extremely slow, ugly or beautiful, white or black? Are you not aware that in all those cases the most extreme at either end are rare and few, but those in between are many and plentiful?

Certainly, I said.

b   Therefore, he said, if a contest of wickedness were established, there too the winners, you think, would be very few?

That is likely, said I.

Likely indeed, he said, but arguments are not like men in this particular. I was merely following your lead just now.[16] The similarity lies rather in this: it is as when one who lacks skill in arguments puts his trust in an argument as being true, then shortly afterwards believes

---

16. Socrates presumably means that there are plenty of very bad arguments. It is not clear where he was following Phaedo in the argument.

it to be false—as sometimes it is and sometimes it is not—and so with another argument and then another. You know how those in particular who spend their time studying contradiction in the end believe them- selves to have become very wise and that they alone have understood   c that there is no soundness or reliability in any object or in any argu- ment, but that all that exists simply fluctuates up and down as if it were in the Euripus[17] and does not remain in the same place for any time at all.

What you say, I said, is certainly true.

It would be pitiable, Phaedo, he said, when there is a true and reliable argument and one that can be understood, if a man who has dealt with such arguments as appear at one time true, at another time untrue,   d should not blame himself or his own lack of skill but, because of his distress, in the end gladly shift the blame away from himself to the argu- ments, and spend the rest of his life hating and reviling reasonable dis- cussion and so be deprived of truth and knowledge of reality.

Yes, by Zeus, I said, that would be pitiable indeed.

This then is the first thing we should guard against, he said. We should not allow into our minds the conviction that argumentation has   e nothing sound about it; much rather we should believe that it is we who are not yet sound and that we must take courage and be eager to attain soundness, you and the others for the sake of your whole life still to come, and I for the sake of death itself. I am in danger at this   91 moment of not having a philosophical attitude about this, but like those who are quite uneducated, I am eager to get the better of you in argu- ment, for the uneducated, when they engage in argument about any- thing, give no thought to the truth about the subject of discussion but are only eager that those present will accept the position they have set forth. I differ from them only to this extent: I shall not be eager to get the agreement of those present that what I say is true, except inci- dentally, but I shall be very eager that I should myself be thoroughly convinced that things are so. For I am thinking—see in how conten- tious a spirit—that if what I say is true, it is a fine thing to be con- vinced; if, on the other hand, nothing exists after death, at least for   b this time before I die I shall distress those present less with lamenta- tions and my folly will not continue to exist along with me—that would be a bad thing—but will come to an end in a short time. Thus

---

17. The Euripus was the name of the straits between Euboea and Boetia; its cur- rents were both violent and variable.

prepared, Simmias and Cebes, he said, I come to deal with your argument. If you will take my advice, you will give but little thought to
c   Socrates but much more to the truth. If you think that what I say is true, agree with me; if not, oppose it with every argument and take care that in my eagerness I do not deceive myself and you and, like a bee, leave my sting in you when I go.

We must proceed, he said, and first remind me of what you said if I do not appear to remember it. Simmias, as I believe, is in doubt and fears that the soul, though it is more divine and beautiful than the
d   body, yet predeceases it, being a kind of harmony. Cebes, I thought, agrees with me that the soul lasts much longer than the body, but that no one knows whether the soul often wears out many bodies and then, on leaving its last body, is now itself destroyed. This then is death, the destruction of the soul, since the body is always being destroyed. Are these the questions, Simmias and Cebes, which we must investigate?

e   They both agreed that they were.

Do you then, he asked, reject all our previous statements, or some but not others?

Some, they both said, but not others.

What, he said, about the statement we made that learning is recollection and that, if this was so, our soul must of necessity exist elsewhere
92 before us, before it was imprisoned in the body?

For myself, said Cebes, I was wonderfully convinced by it at the time and I stand by it now also, more than by any other statement.

That, said Simmias, is also my position, and I should be very surprised if I ever changed my opinion about this.

But you must change your opinion, my Theban friend, said Socrates, if you still believe that a harmony is a composite thing, and that the soul is a kind of harmony of the elements of the body in a state of tension, for surely you will not allow yourself to maintain that a com-
b   posite harmony existed before those elements from which it had to be composed, or would you?

Never, Socrates, he said.

Do you realize, he said, that this is what you are in fact saying when you state that the soul exists before it takes on the form and body of a man and that it is composed of elements which do not yet exist? A harmony is not like that to which you compare it; the lyre and the strings and the notes, though still unharmonized, exist; the harmony is com-
c   posed last of all, and is the first to be destroyed. How will you harmonize this statement with your former one?

In no way, said Simmias.

And surely, he said, a statement about harmony should do so more than any other.

It should, said Simmias.

So your statement is inconsistent? Consider which of your statements you prefer, that learning is recollection or that the soul is a harmony.

I much prefer the former, Socrates. I adopted the latter without proof, because of a certain probability and plausibility, which is why it appeals to most men. I know that arguments of which the proof is based on probability are pretentious and, if one does not guard against them, they certainly deceive one, in geometry and everything else. The theory of recollection and learning, however, was based on an assumption worthy of acceptance, for our soul was said to exist also before it came into the body, just as the reality that is of the kind that we qualify by the words "what it is," and I convinced myself that I was quite correct to accept it. Therefore, I cannot accept the theory that the soul is a harmony either from myself or anyone else.

d

e

What of this, Simmias? Do you think it natural for a harmony, or any other composite, to be in a different state from that of the elements of which it is composed?

93

Not at all, said Simmias.

Nor, as I think, can it act or be acted upon in a different way than its elements?

He agreed.

One must therefore suppose that a harmony does not direct its components, but is directed by them.

He accepted this.

A harmony is therefore far from making a movement, or uttering a sound, or doing anything else, in a manner contrary to that of its parts.

Far from it indeed, he said.

Does not the nature of each harmony depend on the way it has been harmonized?

I do not understand, he said.

Will it not, if it is more and more fully harmonized, be more and more fully a harmony, and if it is less and less fully harmonized, it will be less and less fully a harmony?

b

Certainly.

Can this be true about the soul, that one soul is more and more fully a soul than another, or is less and less fully a soul, even to the smallest extent?

Not in any way.

Come now, by Zeus, he said. One soul is said to have intelligence and virtue and to be good, another to have folly and wickedness and to be bad. Are those things truly said?

They certainly are.

What will someone who holds the theory that the soul is a harmony say that those things are which reside in the soul, that is, virtue and wickedness? Are these some other harmony and disharmony? That the good soul is harmonized and, being a harmony, has within itself another harmony, whereas the evil soul is both itself a lack of harmony and has no other within itself?

I don't know what to say, said Simmias, but one who holds that assumption must obviously say something of that kind.

We have previously agreed, he said, that one soul is not more and not less a soul than another, and this means that one harmony is not more and more fully, or less and less fully, a harmony than another. Is that not so?

Certainly.

Now that which is no more and no less a harmony is not more or less harmonized. Is that so?

It is.

Can that which is neither more nor less harmonized partake more or less of harmony, or does it do so equally?

Equally.

Then if a soul is neither more nor less a soul than another, it has been harmonized to the same extent?

That is so.

If that is so, it would have no greater share of disharmony or of harmony?

It would not.

That being the case, could one soul have more wickedness or virtue than another, if wickedness is disharmony and virtue harmony?

It could not.

But rather, Simmias, according to correct reasoning, no soul, if it is a harmony, will have any share of wickedness, for harmony is surely

altogether this very thing, harmony, and would never share in disharmony.

It certainly would not.

Nor would a soul, being altogether this very thing, a soul, share in
wickedness?

How could it, in view of what has been said?

So it follows from this argument that all the souls of all living
creatures will be equally good, if souls are by nature equally this very
thing, souls.

I think so, Socrates.

Does our argument seem right, he said, and does it seem that it
should have come to this, if the hypothesis that the soul is a harmony   b
was correct?

Not in any way, he said.

Further, of all the parts of a man, can you mention any other part
that rules him than his soul, especially if it is a wise soul?

I cannot.

Does it do so by following the affections of the body or by opposing
them? I mean, for example, that when the body is hot and thirsty the
soul draws him to the opposite, to not drinking; when the body is hungry, to not eating, and we see a thousand other examples of the soul
opposing the affections of the body. Is that not so?   c

It certainly is.

On the other hand we previously agreed that if the soul were a harmony, it would never be out of tune with the stress and relaxation
and the striking of the strings or anything else done to its composing
elements, but that it would follow and never direct them?

We did so agree, of course.

Well, does it now appear to do quite the opposite, ruling over all
the elements of which one says it is composed, opposing nearly all of   d
them throughout life, directing all their ways, inflicting harsh and pain-
ful punishment on them, at times in physical culture and medicine, at
other times more gently by threats and exhortations, holding converse
with desires and passions and fears as if it were one thing talking to a
different one, as Homer wrote somewhere in the *Odyssey* where he says
that Odysseus "struck his breast and rebuked his heart, saying,

> 'Endure, my heart, you have endured worse than this'"?

Do you think that when he composed this the poet thought that   e his soul was a harmony, a thing to be directed by the affections of the body? Did he not rather regard it as ruling over them and mastering them, itself a much more divine thing than a harmony?

Yes, by Zeus, I think so, Socrates.

Therefore, my good friend, it is quite wrong for us to say that the soul is a harmony, and in saying so we would disagree both with the divine poet Homer and with ourselves.

That is so, he said.

Very well, said Socrates. Harmonia of Thebes seems somehow reasonably propitious to us. How and by what argument, my dear Cebes, can we propitiate Cadmus?[18]

I think, Cebes said, that you will find a way. You dealt with the argument about harmony in a manner that was quite astonishing to me. When Simmias was speaking of his difficulties I was very much wondering whether anyone would be able to deal with his argument, and I was quite dumbfounded when, right away he could not resist your argument's first onslaught. I should not wonder therefore if that of Cadmus suffered the same fate.

My good sir, said Socrates, do not boast, lest some malign influence upset the argument we are about to make. However, we leave that to the care of the god, but let us come to grips with it in the Homeric fashion, to see if there is anything in what you say. The sum of your problem is this: you consider that the soul must be proved to be immortal and indestructible before a philosopher on the point of death, who is confident that he will fare much better in the underworld than if he had led any other kind of life, can avoid being foolish and simple-minded in this confidence. To prove that the soul is strong, that it is divine, that it existed before we were born as men, all this, you say, does not show the soul to be immortal but only long-lasting. That it existed for a very long time before, that it knew much and acted much, makes it no more immortal because of that; indeed, its very entering into a human body was the beginning of its destruction, like a disease; it would live that life in distress and would in the end be destroyed in what we call death. You say it makes no difference whether it enters a body once or many times as far as the fear of each of us is concerned, for it is natural for a man who is no fool to be afraid, if he does not

---

18. Harmonia was in legend the wife of Cadmus, the founder of Thebes. Socrates' punning joke is simply that, having dealt with Harmonia (harmony), we must now deal with Cadmus (i.e., Cebes, the other Theban).

know and cannot prove that the soul is immortal. This, I think, is what you maintain, Cebes; I deliberately repeat it often, in order that no point may escape us, and that you may add or subtract something if you wish.

And Cebes said: "There is nothing that I want to add or subtract at the moment. That is what I say."

Socrates paused for a long time, deep in thought. He then said: "This is no unimportant problem that you raise, Cebes, for it requires a thorough investigation of the cause of generation and destruction. I will, if you wish, give you an account of my experience in these matters. Then if something I say seems useful to you, make use of it to persuade us of your position."

I surely do wish that, said Cebes.

Listen then, and I will, Cebes, he said. When I was a young man I was wonderfully keen on that wisdom which they call natural science, for I thought it splendid to know the causes of everything, why it comes to be, why it perishes and why it exists. I was often changing my mind in the investigation, in the first instance, of questions such as these: Are living creatures nurtured when heat and cold produce a kind of putrefaction, as some say? Do we think with our blood, or air, or fire, or none of these, and does the brain provide our senses of hearing and sight and smell, from which come memory and opinion, and from memory and opinion which has become stable, comes knowledge? Then again, as I investigated how these things perish and what happens to things in the sky and on the earth, finally I became convinced that I had no natural aptitude at all for that kind of investigation, and of this I will give you sufficient proof. This investigation made me quite blind even to those things which I and others thought that I clearly knew before, so that I unlearned what I thought I knew before, about many other things and specifically about how men grew. I thought before that it was obvious to anybody that men grew through eating and drinking, for food adds flesh to flesh and bones to bones, and in the same way appropriate parts were added to all other parts of the body, so that the man grew from an earlier small bulk to a large bulk later, and so a small man became big. That is what I thought then. Do you not think it was reasonable?

I do, said Cebes.

Then further consider this: I thought my opinion was satisfactory, that when a large man stood by a small one he was taller by a head, and so a horse was taller than a horse. Even clearer than this, I thought that ten was more than eight because two had been added, and that a two-cubit length is larger than a cubit because it surpasses it by half its length.

And what do you think now about those things?

That I am far, by Zeus, from believing that I know the cause of any of those things. I will not even allow myself to say that where one is added to one either the one to which it is added or the one that is added becomes two, or that the one added and the one to which it is added become two because of the addition of the one to the other. I wonder that, when each of them is separate from the other, each of them is one, nor are they then two, but that, when they come near to one another, this is the cause of their becoming two, the coming together and being placed closer to one another. Nor can I any longer be persuaded that when one thing is divided, this division is the cause of its becoming two, for just now the cause of becoming two was the opposite. At that time it was their coming close together and one was added to the other, but now it is because one is taken and separated from the other.

I do not any longer persuade myself that I know why a unit or anything else comes to be, or perishes or exists by the old method of investigation, and I do not accept it, but I have a confused method of my own. One day I heard someone reading, as he said, from a book of Anaxagoras, and saying that it is Mind that directs and is the cause of everything. I was delighted with this cause and it seemed to me good, in a way, that Mind should be the cause of all. I thought that if this were so, the directing Mind would direct everything and arrange each thing in the way that was best. If then one wished to know the cause of each thing, why it comes to be or perishes or exists, one had to find what was the best way for it to be, or to be acted upon, or to act. On these premises then it befitted a man to investigate only, about this and other things, what is best. The same man must inevitably also know what is worse, for that is part of the same knowledge. As I reflected on this subject I was glad to think that I had found in Anaxagoras a teacher about the cause of things after my own heart, and that he would tell me, first, whether the earth is flat or round, and then would explain why it is so of necessity, saying which is better, and that it was better to be so. If he said it was in the middle of the universe, he would go on to show that it was better for it to be in the middle, and if he showed me those things I should be prepared never to desire any other kind of cause. I was ready to find out in the same way about the sun and the moon and the other heavenly bodies, about their relative speed, their turnings and whatever else happened to them, how it is best that each should act or be acted upon. I never thought that Anaxagoras, who said that those things were directed by Mind, would bring in any other cause for them than that it was best for them to be as they are. Once he had given the best for each as the cause for each and the general cause of all, I thought he would go on to explain the common good for all, and I would not have exchanged my hopes for a fortune. I eagerly acquired his books and read them as quickly as I could in order to know the best and the worst as soon as possible.

This wonderful hope was dashed as I went on reading and saw that the man made no use of Mind, nor gave it any responsibility for the management of things, but mentioned as causes air and ether and water and many other strange things. That seemed to me much like saying that Socrates' actions are all due to his mind, and then in trying to tell the causes of everything I do, to say that the reason that I am sitting here is because my body consists of bones and sinews, because the bones are hard and are separated by joints, that the sinews are such as to contract and relax, that they surround the bones along with flesh and skin which hold them together, then as the bones are hanging in their sockets, the relaxation and contraction of the sinews enable me to bend my limbs, and that is the cause of my sitting here with my limbs bent.

Again, he would mention other such causes for my talking to you: sounds and air and hearing, and a thousand other such things, but he would neglect to mention the true causes, that, after the Athenians decided it was better to condemn me, for this reason it seemed best to me to sit here and more right to remain and to endure whatever penalty they ordered. For by the dog, I think these sinews and bones could long ago have been in Megara or among the Boeotians, taken there by my belief as to the best course, if I had not thought it more right and honourable to endure whatever penalty the city ordered rather than escape and run away. To call those things causes is too absurd. If someone said that without bones and sinews and all such things, I should not be able to do what I decided, he would be right, but surely to say that they are the cause of what I do, and not that I have chosen the best course, even though I act with my mind, is to speak very lazily and carelessly. Imagine not being able to distinguish the real cause from that without which the cause would not be able to act as a cause. It is what the majority appear to do, like people groping in the dark;

they call it a cause, thus giving it a name that does not belong to it. That is why one man surrounds the earth with a vortex to make the heavens keep it in place, another makes the air support it like a wide

c lid. As for their capacity of being in the best place they could possibly be put, this they do not look for, nor do they believe it to have any divine force, but they believe that they will some time discover a stronger and more immortal Atlas to hold everything together more, and they do not believe that the truly good and "binding" binds and holds them together. I would gladly become the disciple of any man who taught the workings of that kind of cause. However, since I was deprived and could neither discover it myself nor learn it from

d another, do you wish me to give you an explanation of how, as a second best, I busied myself with the search for the cause, Cebes?

I would wish it above all else, he said.

After this, he said, when I had wearied of investigating things, I thought that I must be careful to avoid the experience of those who watch an eclipse of the sun, for some of them ruin their eyes unless they watch its reflection in water or some such material. A similar

e thought crossed my mind, and I feared that my soul would be alto-gether blinded if I looked at things with my eyes and tried to grasp them with each of my senses. So I thought I must take refuge in discus-sions and investigate the truth of things by means of words. However, perhaps this analogy is inadequate, for I certainly do not admit that

100 one who investigates things by means of words is dealing with images any more than one who looks at facts. However, I started in this man-ner: taking as my hypothesis in each case the theory that seemed to me the most compelling, I would consider as true, about cause and every-thing else, whatever agreed with this, and as untrue whatever did not so agree. But I want to put my meaning more clearly for I do not think that you understand me now.

No, by Zeus, said Cebes, not very well.

b This, he said, is what I mean. It is nothing new, but what I have never stopped talking about, both elsewhere and in the earlier part of our conversation. I am going to try to show you the kind of cause with which I have concerned myself. I turn back to those oft-mentioned things and proceed from them. I assume the existence of a Beautiful, itself by itself, of a Good and a Great and all the rest. If you grant me these and agree that they exist, I hope to show you the cause as a result, and to find the soul to be immortal.

Take it that I grant you this, said Cebes, and hasten to your c
conclusion.

Consider then, he said, whether you share my opinion as to what follows, for I think that, if there is anything beautiful besides the Beautiful itself, it is beautiful for no other reason than that it shares in that
Beautiful, and I say so with everything. Do you agree to this sort of
cause? — I do.

I no longer understand or recognize those other sophisticated
causes, and if someone tells me that a thing is beautiful because it has a d
bright colour or shape or any such thing, I ignore these other reasons—for all these confuse me—but I simply, naively and perhaps
foolishly cling to this, that nothing else makes it beautiful other than
the presence of, or the sharing in, or however you may describe its
relationship to that Beautiful we mentioned, for I will not insist on
the precise nature of the relationship, but that all beautiful things are
beautiful by the Beautiful. That, I think, is the safest answer I can give
myself or anyone else. And if I stick to this I think I shall never fall e
into error. This is the safe answer for me or anyone else to give,
namely, that it is through Beauty that beautiful things are made beautiful. Or do you not think so too?—I do.

And that it is through Bigness that big things are big and the bigger are bigger, and that smaller things are made small by Smallness? —
Yes.

And you would not accept the statement that one man is taller than
another by a head[19] and the shorter man shorter by the same, but you 101
would bear witness that you mean nothing else than that everything
that is bigger is made bigger by nothing else than by Bigness, and that
is the cause of its being bigger, and the smaller is made smaller only by
Smallness and this is why it is smaller. I think you would be afraid that
some opposite argument would confront you if you said that someone
is bigger or smaller by a head, first, because the bigger is bigger and
the smaller smaller by the same, then because the bigger is bigger by a
head which is small, and this would be strange, namely, that someone b
is made bigger by something small. Would you not be afraid of this?

---

19. This is very puzzling in English. In Greek the confusion is due to the double
use of the dative, instrumental and causal, so that it could mean, "because of a head,"
which is nonsense of course, but the ambiguity is there and makes the statement of
Socrates possible.

I certainly would, said Cebes, laughing.

Then you would be afraid to say that ten is more than eight by two, and that this is the cause of the excess, and not magnitude and because of magnitude, or that two cubits is bigger than one cubit by half and not by Bigness, for this is the same fear. — Certainly.

c   Then would you not avoid saying that when one is added to one it is the addition and when it is divided it is the division that is the cause of two? And you would loudly exclaim that you do not know how else each thing can come to be except by sharing in the particular reality in which it shares, and in these cases you do not know of any other cause of becoming two except by sharing in Twoness, and that the things that are to be two must share in this, as that which is to be one must share in Oneness, and you would dismiss these additions and divisions and other such subtleties, and leave them to those wiser than yourself to answer. But you, afraid, as they say, of your own shadow

d   and your inexperience, would cling to the safety of your own hypothesis and give that answer. If someone then attacked your hypothesis itself, you would ignore him and would not answer until you had examined whether the consequences that follow from it agree with one another or contradict one another. And when you must give an account of your hypothesis itself you will proceed in the same way: you will assume another hypothesis, the one which seems to you best of

e   the higher ones until you come to something acceptable, but you will not jumble the two as the debaters do by discussing the hypothesis and its consequences at the same time, if you wish to discover any truth. This they do not discuss at all nor give any thought to, but their wisdom enables them to mix everything up and yet to be pleased with

102   themselves, but if you are a philosopher I think you will do as I say.

What you say is very true, said Simmias and Cebes together.

ECHECRATES: Yes, by Zeus, Phaedo, and they were right, I think he made these things wonderfully clear to anyone of even small intelligence.

PHAEDO: Yes indeed, Echecrates, and all those present thought so too.

E: And so do we who were not present but hear of it now. What was said after that?

P: As I recall it, when the above had been accepted, and it was
b   agreed that each of the Forms existed, and that other things acquired their name by having a share in them, he followed this up by asking:

If you say these things are so, when you then say that Simmias is taller than Socrates but shorter than Phaedo, do you not mean that there is in Simmias both tallness and shortness? — I do.

But, he said, do you agree that the words of the statement 'Simmias is taller than Socrates' do not express the truth of the matter? It is not, surely, the nature of Simmias to be taller than Socrates because he is Simmias but because of the tallness he happens to have? Nor is he taller than Socrates because Socrates is Socrates, but because Socrates has smallness compared with the tallness of the other?—True.

Nor is he shorter than Phaedo because Phaedo is Phaedo, but because Phaedo has tallness compared with the shortness of Simmias? — That is so.

So then Simmias is called both short and tall, being between the two, presenting his shortness to be overcome by the tallness of one, and his tallness to overcome the shortness of the other. He smilingly added, I seem to be going to talk like a book, but it is as I say. The other agreed.

My purpose is that you may agree with me. Now it seems to me that not only Tallness itself is never willing to be tall and short at the same time, but also that that tallness in us[20] will never admit the short or be overcome, but one of two things happens: either it flees and retreats whenever its opposite, the short, approaches, or it is destroyed by its approach. It is not willing to endure and admit shortness and be other than it was, whereas I admit and endure shortness and still remain the same person and am this short man. But Tallness, being tall, cannot venture to be small. In the same way, the short in us is unwilling to become or to be tall ever, nor does any other of the opposites become or be its opposite while still being what it was; either it goes away or is destroyed when that happens. — I altogether agree, said Cebes.

When he heard this, someone of those present—I have no clear memory of who it was—said: "By the gods, did we not agree earlier in our discussion[21] to the very opposite of what is now being said,

---

20. The "tallness in us" is not the Form, which is never immanent in the particular, nor need we imagine it to refer to another thing existing between the Form and the particular; it simply refers to the quality of tallness which is clearly inherent in the particulars. The expression could be used without reference to the theory of Forms at all.

21. The reference is to 70d–71a above.

namely, that the larger came from the smaller and the smaller from the larger, and that this simply was how opposites came to be, from their opposites, but now I think we are saying that this would never happen?"

On hearing this, Socrates inclined his head towards the speaker and said: "You have bravely reminded us, but you do not understand the difference between what is said now and what was said then, which was that an opposite thing came from an opposite thing; now we say that the opposite itself could never become opposite to itself, neither that in us or that in nature. Then, my friend, we were talking of things that have opposite qualities and naming these after them, but now we say that these opposites themselves, from the presence of which in them things get their name, never can tolerate the coming to be from one another." At the same time he looked to Cebes and said: "Does anything of what this man says also disturb you?"

Not at the moment, said Cebes, but I do not deny that many things do disturb me.

We are altogether agreed then, he said, that an opposite will never be opposite to itself. — Entirely agreed.

Consider then whether you will agree to this further point. There is something you call hot and something you call cold. — There is.

Are they the same as what you call snow and fire? — By Zeus, no.

So the hot is something other than fire, and the cold is something other than snow? — Yes.

You think, I believe, that being snow it will not admit the hot, as we said before, and remain what it was and be both snow and hot, but when the hot approaches it will either retreat before it or be destroyed. — Quite so.

So fire, as the cold approaches, will either go away or be destroyed; it will never venture to admit coldness and remain what it was, fire and cold. — What you say is true.

It is true then about some of these things that not only the Form itself deserves its own name for all time, but there is something else that is not the Form but has its character whenever it exists. Perhaps I can make my meaning clearer: the Odd must always be given this name we now mention. Is that not so? — Certainly.

Is it the only one of existing things to be called odd?—this is my question—or is there something else than the Odd which one must nevertheless also always call odd, as well as by its own name, because it is such by nature as never to be separated from the Odd? I mean, for example, the number three and many others. Consider three: do you not think that it must always be called both by its own name and by that of the Odd, which is not the same as three? That is the nature of three, and of five, and of half of all the numbers; each of them is odd, but it is not the Odd. Then again, two and four and the whole other b column of numbers; each of them, while not being the same as the Even, is always even. Do you not agree? — Of course.

Look now. What I want to make clear is this: not only do those opposites not admit each other, but this is also true of those things which, while not being opposite to each other yet always contain the opposites, and it seems that these do not admit that Form which is opposite to that which is in them; when it approaches them, they either perish or give way. Shall we not say that three will perish or c undergo anything before, while remaining three, becoming even? — Certainly, said Cebes.

Yet surely two is not the opposite of three? — Indeed it is not.

It is then not only opposite Forms that do not admit each other's approach, but also some other things that do not admit the onset of opposites. — Very true.

Do you then want us, if we can, to define what these are? — I surely do.

Would they be the things that compel whatever they occupy not only d to contain their Form but also always that of some opposite? — How do you mean?

As we were saying just now, you surely know that what the Form of three occupies must be not only three but also odd. — Certainly.

And we say that the opposite Form to the Form that achieves this result could never come to it. — It could not.

Now it is Oddness that has done this? — Yes.

And opposite to this is the Form of the Even? — Yes.

So then the Form of the Even will never come to three? — Never. e

Then three has no share in the Even? — Never.

So three is uneven? — Yes.

As for what I said we must define, that is, what kind of things, while not being opposites to something, yet do not admit the opposite, as for example the triad, though it is not the opposite of the Even, yet does not admit it because it always brings along the opposite of the Even,

105   and so the dyad in relation to the Odd, fire to the Cold, and very many
other things, see whether you would define it thus: Not only does the
opposite not admit its opposite, but that which brings along some opposite into that which it occupies, that which brings this along will not
admit the opposite to that which it brings along. Refresh your memory,
it is no worse for being heard often. Five does not admit the form of
the Even, nor will ten, its double, admit the form of the Odd. It is the
opposite of something else, yet it will not admit the form of the Odd.
Nor does one-and-a-half and other such fractions admit the form of the
b   Whole, nor will one-third, and so on, if you follow me and agree to
this.

I certainly agree, he said, and I follow you.

Tell me again from the beginning, he said, and do not answer in
the words of the question, but do as I do. I say that beyond that safe
answer, which I spoke of first, I see another safe answer. If you should
ask me what, coming into a body, makes it hot, my reply would not be
c   that safe and ignorant one, that it is heat, but our present argument
provides a more sophisticated answer, namely, fire, and if you ask me
what, on coming into a body, makes it sick, I will not say sickness but
fever. Nor, if asked the presence of what in a number makes it odd, I
will not say oddness but oneness, and so with other things. See if you
now sufficiently understand what I want. — Quite sufficiently.

Answer me then, he said, what is it that, present in a body, makes it
living? — A soul.
d   And is that always so? — Of course.

Whatever the soul occupies, it always brings life to it? — It does.

Is there, or is there not, an opposite to life? — There is.

What is it? — Death.

So the soul will never admit the opposite of that which it brings
along, as we agree from what has been said?

Most certainly, said Cebes.

Well, and what do we call that which does not admit the form of the
even? — The uneven.

What do we call that which will not admit the just and that which will
not admit the musical?
e   The unmusical, and the other the unjust.

Very well, what do we call that which does not admit death?

The deathless, he said.

Now the soul does not admit death? — No.

So the soul is deathless? — It is.

Very well, he said. Shall we say that this has been proved, do you think?

Quite adequately proved, Socrates.

Well now, Cebes, he said, if the uneven were of necessity indestructible, surely three would be indestructible? — Of course. 106

And if the non-hot were of necessity indestructible, then whenever anyone brought heat to snow, the snow would retreat safe and unthawed, for it could not be destroyed, nor again could it stand its ground and admit the heat? — What you say is true.

In the same way, if the non-cold were indestructible, then when some cold attacked the fire, it would neither be quenched nor destroyed, but retreat safely. — Necessarily.

Must then the same not be said of the deathless? If the deathless is b also indestructible, it is impossible for the soul to be destroyed when death comes upon it. For it follows from what has been said that it will not admit death or be dead, just as three, we said, will not be even nor will the odd; nor will fire be cold, nor the heat that is in the fire. But, someone might say, what prevents the odd, while not becoming even as has been agreed, from being destroyed, and the even to come to be c instead? We could not maintain against the man who said this that it is not destroyed, for the uneven is not indestructible. If we had agreed that it was indestructible we could easily have maintained that at the coming of the even, the odd and the three have gone away and the same would hold for fire and the hot and the other things. — Surely.

And so now, if we are agreed that the deathless is indestructible, the soul, besides being deathless, is indestructible. If not, we need another d argument.

— There is no need for one as far as that goes, for hardly anything could resist destruction if the deathless, which lasts forever, would admit destruction.

All would agree, said Socrates, that the god, and the Form of life itself, and anything that is deathless, are never destroyed. — All men would agree, by Zeus, to that, and the gods, I imagine, even more so.

If the deathless is indestructible, then the soul, if it is deathless, e would also be indestructible? — Necessarily.

Then when death comes to man, the mortal part of him dies, it seems, but his deathless part goes away safe and indestructible, yielding the place to death. — So it appears.

Therefore the soul, Cebes, he said, is most certainly deathless and indestructible and our souls will really dwell in the underworld.

— I have nothing more to say against that, Socrates, said Cebes, nor can I doubt your arguments. If Simmias here or someone else has something to say, he should not remain silent, for I do not know to what further occasion other than the present he could put it off if he wants to say or to hear anything on these subjects.

Certainly, said Simmias, I myself have no remaining grounds for doubt after what has been said; nevertheless, in view of the importance of our subject and my low opinion of human weakness, I am bound still to have some private misgivings about what we have said.

You are not only right to say this, Simmias, Socrates said, but our first hypotheses require clearer examination, even though we find them convincing. And if you analyze them adequately, you will, I think, follow the argument as far as a man can and if the conclusion is clear, you will look no further. — That is true.

It is right to think then, gentlemen, that if the soul is immortal, it requires our care not only for the time we call our life, but for the sake of all time, and that one is in terrible danger if one does not give it that care. If death were escape from everything, it would be a great boon to the wicked to get rid of the body and of their wickedness together with their soul. But now that the soul appears to be immortal, there is no escape from evil or salvation for it except by becoming as good and wise as possible, for the soul goes to the underworld possessing nothing but its education and upbringing, which are said to bring the greatest benefit or harm to the dead right at the beginning of the journey yonder.

We are told that when each person dies, the guardian spirit who was allotted to him in life proceeds to lead him to a certain place, whence those who have been gathered together there must, after being judged, proceed to the underworld with the guide who has been appointed to lead them thither from here. Having there undergone what they must and stayed there the appointed time, they are led back here by another guide after long periods of time. The journey is not as Aeschylus' Tele-phus[22] describes it. He says that only one single path leads to Hades,

---

22. The *Telephus* of Aeschylus is not extant, and little is known about it.

but I think it is neither one nor simple, for then there would be no need of guides; one could not make any mistake if there were but one path. As it is, it is likely to have many forks and crossroads; and I base this judgement on the sacred rites and customs here.

The well-ordered and wise soul follows the guide and is not without familiarity with its surroundings, but the soul that is passionately attached to the body, as I said before, hovers around it and the visible world for a long time, struggling and suffering much until it is led b away by force and with difficulty by its appointed spirit. When the impure soul which has performed some impure deed joins the others after being involved in unjust killings, or committed other crimes which are akin to these and are actions of souls of this kind, everybody shuns it and turns away, unwilling to be its fellow-traveller or its guide; such a soul wanders alone completely at a loss until a certain time arrives and c it is forcibly led to its proper dwelling place. On the other hand, the soul that has led a pure and moderate life finds fellow-travellers and gods to guide it, and each of them dwells in a place suited to it.

There are many strange places upon the earth, and the earth itself is not such as those who are used to discourse upon it believe it to be in nature or size, as someone has convinced me.

Simmias said: "What do you mean, Socrates? I have myself heard d many things said about the earth, but certainly not the things that convince you. I should be glad to hear them."

Indeed, Simmias, I do not think it requires the skill of Glaucus[23] to tell you what they are, but to prove them true requires more than that skill, and I should perhaps not be able to do so. Also, even if I had the knowledge, my remaining time would not be long enough to tell the tale. However, nothing prevents my telling you what I am convinced is e the shape of the earth and what its regions are.

Even that is sufficient, said Simmias.

Well then, he said, the first thing of which I am convinced is that if the earth is a sphere in the middle of the heavens, it has no need of air 109 or any other force to prevent it from falling. The homogeneous nature of the heavens on all sides and the earth's own equipoise are sufficient to hold it, for an object balanced in the middle of something

---

23. A proverbial expression meaning that a difficult task required the skill of Glaucus. Its origin is obscure, for there are several explanations given by the Scholiasts.

homogeneous will have no tendency to incline more in any direction than any other but will remain unmoved. This, he said, is the first point of which I am persuaded.

And rightly so, said Simmias.

Further, the earth is very large, and we live around the sea in a small
b   portion of it between Phasis and the pillars of Heracles, like ants or frogs around a swamp; many other peoples live in many such parts of it. Everywhere about the earth there are numerous hollows of many kinds and shapes and sizes into which the water and the mist and the air have gathered. The earth itself is pure and lies in the pure sky where the stars are situated, which the majority of those who discourse
c   on these subjects call the ether. The water and mist and air are the sediment of the ether and they always flow into the hollows of the earth. We, who dwell in the hollows of it, are unaware of this and we think that we live above, on the surface of the earth. It is as if someone who lived deep down in the middle of the ocean thought he was living on its surface. Seeing the sun and the other heavenly bodies through
d   the water, he would think the sea to be the sky; because he is slow and weak, he has never reached the surface of the sea or risen with his head above the water or come out of the sea to our region here, nor seen how much purer and more beautiful it is than his own region, nor has he ever heard of it from anyone who has seen it.

Our experience is the same: living in a certain hollow of the earth, we believe that we live upon its surface; the air we call the heavens, as if the stars made their way through it; this too is the same: because of our weakness and slowness we are not able to make our way to the
e   upper limit of the air; if anyone got to this upper limit, if anyone came to it or reached it on wings and his head rose above it, then just as fish on rising from the sea see things in our region, he would see things there and, if his nature could endure to contemplate them, he would know that there is the true heaven, the true light and the true earth,
110 for the earth here, these stones and the whole region, are spoiled and eaten away, just as things in the sea are by the salt water.

Nothing worth mentioning grows in the sea, nothing, one might say, is fully developed; there are caves and sand and endless slime and mud wherever there is earth—not comparable in any way with the beauties of our region. So those things above are in their turn far superior to the things we know. Indeed, if this is the moment to tell a tale,
b   Simmias, it is worth hearing about the nature of things on the surface of the earth under the heavens.

At any rate, Socrates, said Simmias, we should be glad to hear this story.

Well then, my friend, in the first place it is said that the earth, looked at from above, looks like those spherical balls made up of twelve pieces of leather; it is multi-coloured, and of these colours those used by our painters give us an indication; up there the whole earth has these colours, but much brighter and purer than these; one part is c sea-green and of marvelous beauty, another is golden, another is white, whiter than chalk or snow; the earth is composed also of the other colours, more numerous and beautiful than any we have seen. The very hollows of the earth, full of water and air, gleaming among the variety of other colours, present a colour of their own so that the d whole is seen as a continuum of variegated colours. On the surface of the earth the plants grow with corresponding beauty, the trees and the flowers and the fruits, and so with the hills and the stones, more beautiful in their smoothness and transparency and colour. Our precious stones here are but fragments, our cornelians, jaspers, emeralds and the rest. All stones there are of that kind, and even more beautiful. The e reason is that there they are pure, not eaten away or spoiled by decay and brine, or corroded by the water and air which have flowed into the hollows here and bring ugliness and disease upon earth, stones, the other animals and plants. The earth itself is adorned with all these things, and also with gold and silver and other metals. These stand 111 out, being numerous and massive and occurring everywhere, so that the earth is a sight for the blessed. There are many other living creatures upon the earth, and also men, some living inland, others at the edge of the air, as we live on the edge of the sea, others again live on islands surrounded by air close to the mainland. In a word, what water and the sea are to us, the air is to them and the ether is to them b what the air is to us. The climate is such that they are without disease, and they live much longer than people do here; their eyesight, hearing and intelligence and all such are as superior to ours as air is superior to water and ether to air in purity; they have groves and temples dedicated to the gods, in which the gods really dwell, and they communicate with them by speech and prophecy and by the sight of them; they c see the sun and moon and stars as they are, and in other ways their happiness is in accord with this.

This then is the nature of the earth as a whole and of its surroundings; around the whole of it there are many regions in the hollows; some are deeper and more open than that in which we live; others are

deeper and have a narrower opening than ours, and there are some
d   that have less depth and more width. All these are connected with each
other below the surface of the earth in many places by narrow and
broader channels, and thus have outlets through which much water
flows from one to another as into mixing bowls; huge rivers of both
hot and cold water thus flow beneath the earth eternally, much fire
and large rivers of fire, and many of wet mud, both more pure and
e   more muddy, such as those flowing in advance of the lava and the
stream of lava itself in Sicily. These streams then fill up every and all
regions as the flow reaches each, and all these places move up and
down with the oscillating movement of the earth. The natural cause
of the oscillation is as follows: one of the hollows of the earth, which
112 is also the biggest, pierces through the whole earth; it is that which
Homer mentioned when he said: "Far down where is the deepest
pit below the earth . . . ," and which he elsewhere, and many other
poets, call Tartarus; into this chasm all the rivers flow together, and
again flow out of it, and each river is affected by the nature of the land
b   through which it flows. The reason for their flowing into and out of
Tartarus is that this water has no bottom or solid base but it oscillates
up and down in waves, and the air and wind about it do the same,
for they follow it when it flows to this or that part of the earth. Just
as when people breathe, the flow of air goes in and out, so here the
air oscillates with the water and creates terrible winds as it goes in and
c   out. Whenever the water retreats to what we call the lower part of the
earth, it flows into those parts and fills them up as if the water were
pumped in; when it leaves that part for this, it fills these parts again,
and the parts filled flow through the channels and through the earth
and in each case arrive at the places to which the channels lead and
create seas and marshes and rivers and springs. From there the waters
d   flow under the earth again, some flowing around larger and more
numerous regions, some round smaller and shallower ones, then flow
back into Tartarus, some at a point much lower than where they issued
forth, others only a little way, but all of them at a lower point, some of
them at the opposite side of the chasm, some on the same side; some
flow in a wide circle round the earth once or many times like snakes,
then go as far down as possible, then go back into the chasm of Tartarus. From each side it is possible to flow down as far as the center,
e   but not beyond, for this part that faces the river flow from either side is
steep.

There are many other large rivers of all kinds, and among these
there are four of note; the biggest which flows on the outside (of the

earth) in a circle is called Oceanus; opposite it and flowing in the opposite direction is the Acheron; it flows through many other deserted regions and further underground makes its way to the Acherousian lake to which the souls of the majority come after death and, after remaining there for a certain appointed time, longer for some, shorter for others, they are sent back to birth as living creatures. The third river issues between the first two, and close to its source it falls into a region burning with much fire and makes a lake larger than our sea, boiling with water and mud. From there it goes in a circle, foul and muddy, and winding on its way it comes, among other places, to the edge of the Acherousian lake but does not mingle with its waters; then, coiling many times underground it flows lower down into Tartarus; this is called the Pyriphlegethon, and its lava streams throw off fragments of it in various parts of the earth. Opposite this the fourth river issues forth, which is called Stygion, and it is said to flow first into a terrible and wild region, all of it blue-gray in colour, and the lake that this river forms by flowing into it is called the Styx. As its waters fall into the lake they acquire dread powers; then diving below and winding round it flows in the opposite direction from the Pyriphlegethon and into the opposite side of the Acherousian lake; its waters do not mingle with any other; it too flows in a circle and into Tartarus opposite the Pyriphlegethon. The name of that fourth river, the poets tell us, is Cocytus.

Such is the nature of these things. When the dead arrive at the place to which each has been led by his guardian spirit, they are first judged as to whether they have led a good and pious life. Those who have lived an average life make their way to the Acheron and embark upon such vessels as there are for them and proceed to the lake. There they dwell and are purified by penalties for any wrongdoing they may have committed; they are also suitably rewarded for their good deeds as each deserves. Those who are deemed incurable because of the enormity of their crimes, having committed many great sacrileges or wicked and unlawful murders and other such wrongs—their fitting fate is to be hurled into Tartarus never to emerge from it. Those who are deemed to have committed great but curable crimes, such as doing violence to their father or mother in a fit of temper but who have felt remorse for the rest of their lives, or who have killed someone in a similar manner, these must of necessity be thrown into Tartarus, but a year later the current throws them out, those who are guilty of murder by way of Cocytus, and those who have done violence to their parents by way of the Pyriphlegethon. After they have been carried along to

118

b

c

d

e

114

the Acherousian lake, they cry out and shout, some for those they have
killed, others for those they have maltreated, and calling them they
then pray to them and beg them to allow them to step out into the lake
and to receive them. If they persuade them, they do step out and their
punishment comes to an end; if they do not, they are taken back into
Tartarus and from there into the rivers, and this does not stop until they
have persuaded those they have wronged, for this is the punishment
which the judges imposed on them.

Those who are deemed to have lived an extremely pious life are
freed and released from the regions of the earth as from a prison; they
make their way up to a pure dwelling place and live on the surface
of the earth. Those who have purified themselves sufficiently by philosophy live in the future altogether without a body; they make their
way to even more beautiful dwelling places which it is hard to describe
clearly, nor do we now have the time to do so. Because of the things we
have enunciated, Simmias, one must make every effort to share in virtue and wisdom in one's life, for the reward is beautiful and the hope is
great.

No sensible man would insist that these things are as I have des-
cribed them, but I think it is fitting for a man to risk the belief—for
the risk is a noble one—that this, or something like this, is true about
our souls and their dwelling places, since the soul is evidently immortal, and a man should repeat this to himself as if it were an incantation,
which is why I have been prolonging my tale. That is the reason why a
man should be of good cheer about his own soul, if during life he has
ignored the pleasures of the body and its ornamentation as of no concern to him and doing him more harm than good, but has seriously
concerned himself with the pleasures of learning, and adorned his
soul not with alien but with its own ornaments, namely, moderation,
righteousness, courage, freedom and truth, and in that state awaits his
journey to the underworld.

Now you, Simmias, Cebes and the rest of you, Socrates continued,
will each take that journey at some other time but my fated day calls
me now, as a tragic character might say, and it is about time for me to
have my bath, for I think it better to have it before I drink the poison
and save the women the trouble of washing the corpse.

When Socrates had said this Crito spoke. Very well, Socrates, what
are your instructions to me and the others about your children or anything else? What can we do that would please you most?—Nothing
new, Crito, said Socrates, but what I am always saying, that you will

please me and mine and yourselves by taking good care of your own selves in whatever you do, even if you do not agree with me now, but if you neglect your own selves, and are unwilling to live following the tracks, as it were, of what we have said now and on previous occasions, you will achieve nothing even if you strongly agree with me at this moment.

We shall be eager to follow your advice, said Crito, but how shall we bury you?

In any way you like, said Socrates, if you can catch me and I do not escape you. And laughing quietly, looking at us, he said: I do not convince Crito that I am this Socrates talking to you here and ordering all I say, but he thinks that I am the thing which he will soon be looking at as a corpse, and so he asks how he shall bury me. I have been saying for some time and at some length that after I have drunk the poison I shall no longer be with you but will leave you to go and enjoy some good fortunes of the blessed, but it seems that I have said all this to him in vain in an attempt to reassure you and myself too. Give a pledge to Crito on my behalf, he said, the opposite pledge to that he gave the jury. He pledged that I would stay, you must pledge that I will not stay after I die, but that I shall go away, so that Crito will bear it more easily when he sees my body being burned or buried and will not be angry on my behalf, as if I were suffering terribly, and so that he should not say at the funeral that he is laying out, or carrying out, or burying Socrates. For know you well, my dear Crito, that to express oneself badly is not only faulty as far as the language goes, but does some harm to the soul. You must be of good cheer, and say you are burying my body, and bury it in any way you like and think most customary.

After saying this he got up and went to another room to take his bath, and Crito followed him and he told us to wait for him. So we stayed, talking among ourselves, questioning what had been said, and then again talking of the great misfortune that had befallen us. We all felt as if we had lost a father and would be orphaned for the rest of our lives. When he had washed, his children were brought to him—two of his sons were small and one was older—and the women of his household came to him. He spoke to them before Crito and gave them what instructions he wanted. Then he sent the women and children away, and he himself joined us. It was now close to sunset, for he had stayed inside for some time. He came and sat down after his bath and conversed for a short while, when the officer of the Eleven came and stood c   by him and said: "I shall not reproach you as I do the others, Socrates. They are angry with me and curse me when obeying the orders of my superiors, I tell them to drink the poison. During the time you have been here I have come to know you in other ways as the noblest, the gentlest and the best man who has ever come here. So now too I know that you will not make trouble for me; you know who is responsible and you will direct your anger against them. You know what message I bring. Fare you well, and try to endure what you must as easily as

d   possible." The officer was weeping as he turned away and went out. Socrates looked up at him and said: "Fare you well also, we shall do as you bid us." And turning to us he said: "How pleasant the man is! During the whole time I have been here he has come in and conversed with me from time to time, a most agreeable man. And how genuinely he now weeps for me. Come, Crito, let us obey him. Let someone bring the poison if it is ready; if not, let the man prepare it."

e   But Socrates, said Crito, I think the sun still shines upon the hills and has not yet set. I know that others drink the poison quite a long time after they have received the order, eating and drinking quite a bit, and some of them enjoy intimacy with their loved ones. Do not hurry; there is still some time.

It is natural, Crito, for them to do so, said Socrates, for they think

117   they derive some benefit from doing this, but it is not fitting for me. I do not expect any benefit from drinking the poison a little later, except to become ridiculous in my own eyes for clinging to life, and be sparing of it when there is none left. So do as I ask and do not refuse me.

Hearing this, Crito nodded to the slave who was standing near him; the slave went out and after a time came back with the man who was to administer the poison, carrying it made ready in a cup. When Socrates saw him he said: "Well, my good man, you are an expert in this, what must one do?"—"Just drink it and walk around until your legs

b   feel heavy, and then lie down and it will act of itself." And he offered the cup to Socrates who took it quite cheerfully, Echecrates, without a tremor or any change of feature or colour, but looking at the man from under his eyebrows as was his wont, asked: "What do you say about pouring a libation from this drink? It is allowed?" —"We only mix as much as we believe will suffice," said the man.

c   I understand, Socrates said, but one is allowed, indeed one must, utter a prayer to the gods that the journey from here to yonder may be fortunate. This is my prayer and may it be so.

And while he was saying this, he was holding the cup, and then drained it calmly and easily. Most of us had been able to hold back our tears reasonably well up till then, but when we saw him drinking it and after he drank it, we could hold them back no longer; my own tears came in floods against my will. So I covered my face. I was weeping for myself, not for him—for my misfortune in being deprived of such a comrade. Even before me, Crito was unable to restrain his tears and got up. Apollodorus had not ceased from weeping before, and at this moment his noisy tears and anger made everybody present break down, except Socrates. "What is this," he said, "you strange fellows. It is mainly for this reason that I sent the women away, to avoid such unseemliness, for I am told one should die in good omened silence. So keep quiet and control yourselves."

His words made us ashamed, and we checked our tears. He walked around, and when he said his legs were heavy he lay on his back as he had been told to do, and the man who had given him the poison touched his body, and after a while tested his feet and legs, pressed hard upon his foot and asked him if he felt this, and Socrates said no. Then he pressed his calves, and made his way up his body and showed us that it was cold and stiff. He felt it himself and said that when the cold reached his heart he would be gone. As his belly was getting cold Socrates uncovered his head—he had covered it—and said—these were his last words—"Crito, we owe a cock to Asclepius;[24] make this offering to him and do not forget."—"It shall be done," said Crito "tell us if there is anything else," but there was no answer. Shortly afterwards Socrates made a movement; the man uncovered him and his eyes were fixed. Seeing this Crito closed his mouth and his eyes.

Such was the end of our comrade, Echecrates, a man who, we would say, was of all those we have known the best, and also the wisest and the most upright.

---

24. A cock was sacrificed to Asclepius by the sick people who slept in his temples, hoping for a cure. Socrates obviously means that death is a cure for the ills of life.